Praise for
Spaghetti for the Soul

"*Spaghetti for the Soul* shows us how to find hope when there's little, love when there's no affection, and life by faith when the world offers none. The read will feed your passion for living more like Christ."

—JOSH D. McDOWELL, author and speaker

"I love Kathy and Ellie, and you will too! In *Spaghetti for the Soul,* they invite us to taste the lives they live—lives of strength and passion. You will be inspired to love more, hope with greater conviction, and live by faith with deeper trust. Give this book a taste test; you won't be disappointed!"

—JENNIFER ROTHSCHILD, author of *Lessons I Learned in the Dark* and *Self Talk Soul Talk* and founder of WomensMinistry.net

"Reading *Spaghetti for the Soul* is like meeting good friends for dinner. Upon arrival you discover they have prepared comfort food for your body and soul food for your heart. Ellie and Kathy combine sparkling wit, poignant biblical insights, authentic emotions, honest questions, and generous portions of hope in this not-to-be-missed feast for the mind and spirit."

—CAROL KENT, speaker and author of *A New Kind of Normal*

"How does one describe two such delectable, incredible women? Kathy Troccoli and Ellie Lofaro are such unique designs of God that, honestly, the girls just defy description. *Spaghetti for the Soul* is their combined effort to speak their hearts to you and to me. They give us windows into their souls and doorways into their hearts as they open their lives to their readers. They are wonderful, amazing, exciting, fascinating, and full of the sweet love of Jesus. You will experience a tantalizing feast when you sit down to read this book. I loved it, I love them, and I have no doubt that you will as well."

—JAN SILVIOUS, author of *Big Girls Don't Whine* and *Foolproofing Your Life*

Spaghetti
for the Soul

Two Italians from Brooklyn Dish on the Life God Gives

Spaghetti
for the Soul

A Feast of Faith, Hope, and Love

Kathy Troccoli
and Ellie Lofaro

WATERBROOK
PRESS

SPAGHETTI FOR THE SOUL
PUBLISHED BY WATERBROOK PRESS
12265 Oracle Boulevard, Suite 200
Colorado Springs, Colorado 80921
A division of Random House Inc.

ISBN 978-1-4000-7162-3

Published in the United States by WaterBrook Multnomah, an imprint of The Doubleday Publishing Group, a division of Random House Inc., New York.

WATERBROOK and its deer colophon are registered trademarks of Random House Inc.

Library of Congress Cataloging-in-Publication Data
Troccoli, Kathy.
    Spaghetti for the soul : a feast of faith, hope, and love / Kathy Troccoli and Ellie Lofaro. — 1st ed.
        p. cm.
    ISBN 978-1-4000-7162-3
  1. Christian women—Religious life. I. Lofaro, Ellie. II. Title.
    BV4527.T78 2008
    248.8'43—dc22

                                        2008010974

Printed in the United States of America
2008—First Edition

10 9 8 7 6 5 4 3 2 1

SPECIAL SALES
Most WaterBrook Multnomah books are available in special quantity discounts when purchased in bulk by corporations, organizations, and special interest groups. Custom imprinting or excerpting can also be done to fit special needs. For information, please e-mail SpecialMarkets@WaterBrook Multnomah.com or call 1-800-603-7051.

It seems apropos to finally dedicate a book to each other.
What a joy (and test of patience) it was to "cook" this spaghetti together.
We celebrate our faith, our enduring friendship, and our deep love of food.

La vita è bella! ▪ Life is beautiful!

Menu

Antipasti ■ Appetizers
Come to the Table

Primi Piatti ■ First Course
Abundant Faith

Secondi Piatti ■ Second Course
Abundant Hope

Piatti Principale ■ Main Course
Abundant Love

Dolce ■ Dessert
Savor Every Bite

Acknowledgments

We want to express our warm gratitude and thanks to the following people:

- Jeanette Thomason—for your genuine excitement and generous support about an Italian-flavored celebration for the soul. Your vision ignited our desire to serve this feast.
- Laura Barker—for deftly and uniquely combining our voices, and for your dedication to the details. You have challenged us, and we are grateful. (We covet your reference resources!)
- Mark Ford and Micah Kandros—for artistry and attitude that made the photo shoot a pleasure.
- Nicole Beckler and Monie Simpkins—for administrative support extraordinaire.
- The team at WaterBrook Multnomah and Random House—thank you for offering your best so that we could offer ours. It has been a wonderful experience.

We are forever indebted to our prayer teams, who carry us forward on their knees. You ladies know who you are. May the Lord repay you a hundredfold.

We also thank Sheri Berrier, Lisamarie Cortez, Katie Zuniga, and Vanessa Maddoux, who poured special ingredients into the spaghetti pot. Thank you for contributing to this labor of love.

Ellie wishes to thank her husband, Frank, and her children, Paris, Jordan, and Capri, who ate a lot of pizza, Chinese food, and cold chicken while this book was being written.

To the God who sets a place for us at His table—we adore You. Thank You for creating us in Your image and for sending Jesus to show us what You look like.

Antipasti ▪ Appetizers

Come to the Table

The trouble with eating Italian food is that
five or six days later you're hungry again.

—GEORGE MILLER

Life Is Like a Bowl of Spaghetti

*L*ike most people, the two of us hold chicken soup and its virtues in high regard. It is the ultimate feel-better food. Just a whiff of its warm fragrance can lift your spirits, especially when you're huddled under the covers in the grip of a miserable cold.

But since we women rarely have the luxury of taking a sick day, we'd like to call your attention to a few of the splendiferous and supreme attributes of our own favorite comfort food: spaghetti. Where chicken soup tends to be held in reserve for a healing moment, we believe the glories of spaghetti are meant to be enjoyed regularly. Let's consider for a minute the marvelous characteristics of this staple of life.

In Praise of Pasta

Spaghetti is *satisfying*. One box goes a long way. A quarter pound of spaghetti piles much higher than a quarter pound of hamburger.

Spaghetti is *nourishing*. It's full of nutritious things like semolina, durum wheat, niacin, and iron. If you can't start your day with a bowl of power cereal, you can certainly end it with a bowl of power spaghetti.

Spaghetti is *fun*. Have you ever watched a baby during his or her first encounter with spaghetti? It's hard to picture a more delightful scene. Even for us adults, just the thought of swirling and slurping the unruly strands with some attempt at decorum brings a grin. We challenge you to feel sad while puckering up to suck in a forkful of linguini.

Spaghetti is *celebratory*. When we Italians dish spaghetti, or any of the broad array of other pasta shapes, from a massive ceramic serving bowl onto the plate of a guest, that is our way of offering our best. We're saying, "Welcome. Sit, eat, be satisfied. We're glad you're here."

Spaghetti is intrinsically *abundant*. It actually grows as it rolls around in the big pot of boiling water. You can eat half of what's in your bowl, yet it still looks just as full as when you started. Sadly, this leads to our next point.

Or Maybe Not

Truth be told, there are a few downsides to spaghetti. Overindulging places us smack in the battle of the bulge. In addition, spaghetti can be messy, sticky, and uncontrollable. And isn't that just like life?

Statistics overwhelmingly resound with the sad and irrefutable fact that many of us feel as if we're tangled up in the slippery strands of life. We have not all found safety, trust, nourishment, and love around our dinner tables, in our homes, or with the people who are supposed to care about us. And some days the only abundance we experience is the weight on our shoulders, the heaviness in our hearts, the loneliness in our daily routines, and the constant pressure to be all things to all people.

Survey today's typical American woman and you'll not need to dig deep to find that she struggles with abundant guilt, frustration, isolation, fatigue, and yes, anger. Where did it all come from? And where can we find something better, something that fills our souls while helping us lose the unnecessary weight of discontent?

In the gospel of John, Jesus declared that one of His reasons for coming to earth was to give people life. More specifically, He came so that we might have life "abundantly" (10:10, NASB). Eugene Peterson's paraphrase of the Bible, The Message, conveys Jesus's intent with these words: "I came so they can have real and eternal life, more and better life than they ever dreamed of."

Real life. *More* life. *Better* life. *Abundant* life. *Eternal* life. Who wouldn't say yes to an offer like that? Where do we sign up? Are there loopholes? What's hidden in the fine print? Isn't this too good to be true?

The two of us are here to say that we *did* sign up and that God has certainly kept His end of the agreement. He has made abundant life available and attainable; our part of the equation is simply to receive what God wants to give.

If you're a bit cynical, wondering if God truly cares about whether or not you have an abundant life, you are not alone. In our travels we meet so many people from all kinds of backgrounds, and we are always excited to find those who truly hunger and thirst after the things of God. But most of the women we encounter seem disillusioned and defeated by life. Many are convinced that God plays favorites or looks the other way when He sees their suffering. Others have placed God in a less-than-attractive box. They view God as too big, too small, too invasive, or too irrelevant. What little faith they cling to has been compartmentalized, politicized, or marginalized.

Oh, do we understand this. We both grew up in families that demonstrated an awareness of the *existence* of God, but not an *experience* of God. Religion came up from time to time—ours was right and everyone else's was wrong—but the topic of knowing God intimately was a big no-no within our immediate and extended families. Heads would shake, eyes would roll, and we were told not to speak of such things because, "It's personal." Yet we were convinced there had to be more to God than à la carte rules and rituals. We both determined to find the "more," wherever our search might lead.

Eventually, it led to both of us as young women asking Jesus to reside in our hearts and to be our constant companion. In these past few decades, as we've enjoyed a romance of sorts with the living God, we have been amazed, thrilled, comforted, and quieted by His goodness and love.

Through the years, however, we occasionally have found ourselves, like so many women we meet, snatching crumbs from the table of God instead of fully participating in the feast that He has prepared and to which He warmly invites each of us. That feast is abundant faith, abundant hope, and abundant love—the essential ingredients of a healthy spiritual and emotional life. The feast is prepared, but we have to make time to enjoy it.

One of our favorite verses in the Scriptures is "Taste and see that the LORD is good" (Psalm 34:8). So we invite you to taste of God's goodness as you join the feast, something we Italians know a whole lot about.

Come Join Our Table

The two of us were born in Brooklyn, and although we didn't meet until adulthood, our childhood memories reflect our shared heritage. For the families in which we grew up, food was far more than a meal. It was an occasion, a feast, a love affair. And if typical weeknight dinners were important, and they were, then Sunday afternoon dinners with our extended families were sacred. Everyone came ready to eat: parents, grandparents, siblings, aunts, uncles, and cousins. No one ever considered skipping out.

An old Italian proverb—*Al tavolo, non sei vecchio*—says, "At the table, we don't grow old." Early in life we each learned a great deal about "the table." At the table, arguments started and ended, marriages were blessed, babies were nibbled on, the departed were cried over, and the living were teased. At the table, you could always find a fresh pot of coffee along with second or third helpings of food, advice, hugs, and sloppy kisses. At the table, all was well with the world.

We have found that every time one of us speaks of the Brooklyn roots and Italian heritage we proudly share, it brings smiles to faces and arouses curiosity. In the pages to follow you'll learn more about us, but for now let's get the usual questions out of the way:

Are all Italians in the Mafia? No, and the inference is unkind, thank you. Watch your back.

Do you really have an uncle Vito and a cousin Vinny? Vito, Vinny, Tony, Dominick, Frank, Johnny, Sal, Paulie, Freddie, Al. Yep, we have 'em all.

Was pasta a daily staple in your home? No, we had steak once a week, chicken twice a week, and pizza on Friday nights.

When did you have your first taste of wine? In church.

Margie's Spaghetti Pie

Consider this Italy's answer to macaroni and cheese!

Ingredients

- 1-pound box spaghetti
- 6 eggs
- 1/2 cup grated Italian cheese, such as parmesan or romano
- 1 cup shredded mozzarella
- 2 tablespoons olive oil, divided

Cooking Instructions

1. Boil spaghetti; strain when al dente (firm).
2. Beat eggs in a large bowl. Add spaghetti and mix well. Add Italian cheese and mix again.
3. Heat 1 tablespoon olive oil in a 12-inch frying pan. Pour in half the spaghetti and heat 3 minutes. Sprinkle mozzarella cheese evenly around, but not to the edges. Add the rest of the spaghetti, then lower heat and fry slowly. When bottom is a bit golden (or crispy, if you prefer), place a flat plate (larger than the pan) over the pan and flip pie onto the plate. If this step frightens you, call someone with strong wrists.
4. Heat the other tablespoon of oil, then slide pie (still upside down) back into frying pan. Heat 5 to 7 more minutes.

Serves 6 as a main course with salad, veggie, and crusty bread. Serves 10 to 12 as side dish.

Is it true that you ate lasagna before turkey on Thanksgiving? Of course. That's why we were thankful.

Did your Sunday afternoon dinners really last four hours? No, sometimes they were five. Italians probably coined the expression "soup to nuts."

Why do Italians only give cash at weddings? The goal is to collect enough for a down payment on a house. The happy couple needs a house to store the truckload of presents they received at the bridal shower.

Why are Italians always arguing? They're not arguing; they're just having loud discussions.

If you have seen the movie *My Big Fat Greek Wedding,* you've seen our families, just with a different accent. Somehow that movie connected with the ethnicity in all of us. Although Nia Vardalos painstakingly and brilliantly portrayed the stereotypical Greco-American family, our southern friends said it was all about *their* relatives, while our Jewish friends claimed it was about *theirs.* For Italian Americans, watching the film was like looking into a huge boot-shaped mirror. Of course, our version would need several minor changes, such as replacing the baklava with cannolis!

As hilarious as that movie was, it also touched poignantly on universal topics that provoke sadness and pain. Who among us doesn't struggle at times with issues of self-esteem and beauty, frustrated dreams, or the craziness of family? We believe that's why the movie was hugely popular: it revealed who we are or, at the least, who we had hoped to be.

Similarly, in the pages that follow we will share many glimpses into *our* lives as we look together at what it means to feast on faith, hope, and love. Some of the stories we tell are joyful, and others are quite painful. We'll look at a few moments we're proud of and others we would really rather forget. No matter what, we will share with honesty because we believe that's how we all grow together.

And how about you and *your* life? Where do you fit into a book about spaghetti and abundance and sticky messes? We're so glad you asked! Whether you are new to the Christian faith or a longtime believer, if you're feeling worn out by life and long to be reenergized and renewed, we invite you to bring a friend, grab a chair, and come to the table. Here you will find understanding, companionship, and abundance to more than satisfy your soul.

Primi Piatti ■ **First Course**

Abundant Faith

*Faith is taking the first step, even when
you don't see the whole staircase.*

—MARTIN LUTHER KING JR.

Chapter 1

Faith That Transforms

Confidence that God is lovingly, actively at work in your world changes everything

My (Kathy's) grandma Troccoli used to make an Italian wedding soup that was out of this world. No one in the family has ever come close to re-creating the flavors that were contained in just one spoonful of this dish. Whenever anyone asked for the recipe, she would say, "I dona knowa. I gowa by feela. A liddle of deesa and a liddle of datta."

Family members recall how it would take her hours and hours to bring this dish to perfection, mixing and rolling the tiny meatballs with tender loving care. The perfect meatball consisted of a certain amount of breadcrumbs, a certain amount of parmesan cheese, and a certain amount of parsley and garlic.

So, too, we've found that a certain combination of ingredients is absolutely vital to a life bursting with flavor. One of these essentials is faith. Walking with an awareness of God's active involvement in our lives can infuse ordinary moments with purpose and passion. Faith enriches our lives with freedom, forgiveness, joy, self-worth, purpose, and confidence. Scientific studies have proven repeatedly that those with deep faith enjoy more-satisfying relationships, less anxiety, better over-all health, and more happiness than those who do not believe in God.

But when we forget about, minimize, or ignore God's role in our lives, it's easy to lose sight of our true purpose. Like novice chefs experimenting in the kitchen, we throw in a little of this and lot of that until we end up with bitter lives, over-seasoned with stress and completely lacking the zest of pure joy.

Tripping Over Our Pedestals of Personal Power

I (Ellie) grew up in a mostly normal, somewhat entertaining, occasionally belli-cose, often denial-ridden Italian American household. If *your* family is dysfunc-tional, take a number; it all goes back to Adam and Eve. Although I made a deliberate choice to follow Jesus at age fifteen, I continued carrying the baggage of childhood around for years.

My paternal grandfather was a harsh disciplinarian, and my father, though loving and affectionate, tended to be critical as a result of his own upbringing. So I absorbed the message that I had to jump through certain hoops, do all the right things, and check off the correct boxes in order to please my parents. (I'm not blaming, just explaining.) Eventually, my goal was to please everybody, which explains my *almost*-past predilection of attempting to be all things to all people.

I was a Brownie, then a Girl Scout. I was a four-sport lettered athlete for all four years of high school. (Yes, in the old days we had four sports seasons.) I was a student-council officer. I served on specially appointed committees for the prin-cipal as well as the superintendent. I was crowned homecoming queen. Well, almost. I lost by seven votes, but I'm not bitter.

Later I continued to shine at Boston College, where I graduated magna cum laude with a double major. During my college years I received a prestigious award for being an exemplary Christian. (Woe to those who dare accept such awards.) As my friend Pastor Brett Fuller likes to say, I was "all that and a bag of chips." Or so I thought. My armor had a few chinks. Increasingly, it seemed my determination to please everyone failed to bring happiness to anyone, especially me.

I wonder if you can relate to my chronic sense of frustration and inadequacy. How much stress in your life comes from trying to launch yourself into the role of

Italian Wedding Soup

This isn't Grandma Troccoli's recipe, but it's much easier and your family and friends will feel the love.

Ingredients

- 1 pound chopped or ground meat, shaped into 12 to 18 mini (rounded teaspoon-size) meatballs and fully cooked (See recipe for Mama Mannarino's Meatballs on page 30.)
- 2 (14-ounce) cans beef broth or stock
- 1 (14-ounce) can chicken broth or stock
- 1 (14-ounce) can vegetable broth or stock
- 1/2 bunch escarole or spinach, rinsed well (or 1 box of frozen chopped spinach, thawed and drained)
- 8 ounces acini de pepe or orzo pasta, cooked al dente (firm) and drained
- salt and pepper to taste
- parmesan cheese to taste

Cooking Instructions

1. Place browned meatballs in a 2- or 3-quart pan and cover with beef broth. Simmer 10 minutes.
2. Add other broths and escarole or spinach. Add drained, firm pasta; simmer 8 minutes.
3. Season to taste, ladle into bowls, and sprinkle liberally with cheese.

Serves 6.

Superwoman? Do you feel compelled to not only bring home the pancetta (that's Italian bacon, in case you're wondering) but also turn it into a gourmet meal, while simultaneously preparing your Bible-study lesson, ensuring your third-grader's diorama accurately reflects the flora and fauna of New Zealand, and flipping through a catalog to find a pair of jeans that will lift, support, and minimize in all the right places?

We women have been sold a bill of goods from Hollywood and Madison Avenue. We tend to believe that we can do it all, that we are superheroes in waiting who simply need to claim our own pedestals of personal power. Not convinced of this? Billions are spent each year instructing the American woman in what she needs, wants, and deserves. The solution to all her problems? More! More of what? Everything, of course.

Consider a recent ad line for the Visa card: "The power to get." What we "get" from trying to have it all is more exhaustion, more dissatisfaction, and more stress. Maybe it's time we stop peering over the proverbial fence where the grass is always greener. Those folks have more mosquitoes and a much higher water bill anyway.

The Bible clearly shows that ours is not the first generation of women whose pursuit of more has left it with less of the things that matter most.

Eve pursued enlightenment apart from God's help. Her approach to life was "I see, I want, I get." In chasing after that one more thing she thought would bring satisfaction, she lost everything, including her garden paradise and her intimacy with God.

Rebekah had a marriage made in heaven, but when she did not see her favorite younger son, Jacob, being elevated and celebrated, she deviated from God's perfect plan and took it upon herself to orchestrate His promised blessing. Rebekah's single-minded obsession left her family in shambles.

And then there's Lot's wife. The few brief references to this woman reveal volumes about her attitude toward life. She was addicted to comfort and self-sufficiency and having what she wanted. When God sent an angel to safely deliver her family out of the burning city, she was told not to look back. Her body moved ahead with her husband and daughters, but her heart stayed behind with her possessions. She stepped toward flight but not toward faith. She looked back and was turned into a pillar of salt. Because of her misplaced priorities, she never caught a glimpse of the blessings God had in store.

God included the stories of these women in the Bible to show us the dangers of always reaching for more, and yet so many of us repeat their mistakes today. I know I have. By the time I turned thirty-five, I had been married ten years and was a mommy to three little ones under the age of five. If you are paying attention to these numbers, please also note that by that point in time, I had been walking and talking (and occasionally balking) alongside Jesus for twenty years. But some days I behaved like a spiritual two-year-old. Like Mrs. Lot, I began looking to people and things, rather than to God, for my sense of security and importance. Like Rebekah, I became comfortable making self-serving chess moves in the game of life. Like Eve, I had grown fairly adept at pointing fingers of blame in every direction except my own.

> *Non si vive di solo pane.*
> **One does not live by bread alone.**

God used motherhood to change all that, to make clear my inability to succeed at everything and please everybody. Finally I was forced to review, regroup, and reevaluate what bearing the Word of God *really* had on my attitudes, my decisions, and my priorities. As He did with Moses, the Lord showed me that I was a somebody who needed to become a nobody so that He could demonstrate His specialty of lifting people up in His time and in His way. I didn't need to perform. I didn't need to jump through the hoops and check off the boxes. My only assignment was to please the audience of One, God Almighty. My faith finally grew up, and so did I.

You Gotta Believe It to See It

Every woman who gives in to the temptation to chase after more and put herself in charge of every crisis and opportunity within reach quickly becomes the creator, producer, director, choreographer, executor, and consumer for every holiday, milestone, church event, and family plan. No wonder we're exhausted!

So when you find yourself trapped on the hamster wheel, spinning for all you're worth, faith becomes your exit ramp—not faith in your own abilities, but faith in a God who sees you, hears you, knows you, understands you, and loves you. This is the God who will walk with you and talk with you and hold your hand through the dark valleys. He will cover you, protect you, and bring you higher to the mountaintops of unspeakable peace and joy. He is the God who has conquered all that frightens you. He is the God who will return to bring you to paradise. He loves you with an everlasting love. He has given His all so that you can share in His amazing promises to those who return His love.

So what will our lives look like when we have the faith to let a loving, caring,

Let's *Dish* About...
When Faith Isn't Easy

EL: Kathy, what do you do when your faith needs a boost?

KT: You know, I can't believe how profoundly conversations filled with words of life affect my spirit. It just happened the other day. I was feeling a little melancholy, overwhelmed by the quietness of my house after the excitement of recent time with family and friends. Then *you* happened to call just when I needed a reminder that my life matters.

In the middle of my "does anybody care?" days, I'll often seek out people who can draw me out of my cave of self-absorption or self-pity by giving me words of life. What a difference it makes to talk with someone who knows my soul and can remind me of the value of my story. I definitely pursue those conversations, because I know I need them. When I hear those words of life, reminders of what God has done and is doing in me, I actually feel as if a smothering weight is being lifted off of me.

actively involved God guide our days? What does *faith* actually mean? Well, as an English teacher for ten mostly fulfilling years, I taught kids in a New York public high school how to talk and write "good." Along the way, I developed a habit of referring to a most excellent source of the meaning of words. I give you Noah Webster, an American patriot, a renowned scholar, a strong family man, a music lover, and an earnest fellow of deep faith. His dictionary offers concise and helpful information, and I highly recommend it. Here's what he says on the topic at hand:

EL: We have so many voices coming at us daily, constantly sending messages. Just the other day my inbox was full of spam e-mails with subject lines like, "Ellie, are you ashamed of how you look?" and, "Ellie, isn't it time for you to lose weight?" In the midst of this barrage of negativity and stress, there's a sweetness and simplicity in being quiet for a minute or three, to just be still and know that He is God, as Psalm 46:10 reminds us to do.

It takes discipline to turn off all those voices and get alone with God, and yet what peace it can bring. We tend to underestimate the power of the Word, but just think: the God who speaks to us from the Bible is the same unchangeable God Almighty who comforted Ruth in her widowhood, who reassured Joseph when he was unjustly imprisoned, who gave Joshua courage as he was about to lead the Israelites across the Jordan River and into the Promised Land. Our consistent and reliable God is speaking to us through His Word, but if we don't turn off those other voices, we miss out on knowing that He is looking at us, that He is hearing our hearts, and that we are absolutely precious to Him.

faith, *n.* unquestioning belief, specifically in God; confidence or trust in a person or thing; a belief that is not based on proof; loyalty; fidelity to one's promise; allegiance

In other words, faith isn't just a matter of acknowledging God's existence. It involves actively placing our confidence in God to keep His promises. It also means demonstrating our allegiance, or commitment, to the purposes toward which He is working in our lives. Romans 1:17 states, "The righteous will live by faith." In other words, faith is not just a noun but a lifestyle. It must penetrate every facet of our lives, not just what we believe or what we do on a Friday night or a Sunday morning. Genuine faith permeates our thoughts, words, and actions from day to day, from moment to moment. No amount of wishful thinking or "I hope so" mentality can substitute for unshakable faith in a God who has promised to deliver us safely to paradise.

Of course, if you are strong and opinionated (like the two of us), you may balk at the part of Webster's definition that says, "a belief that is not based on proof." What is *that* about? You mean we're supposed to trust our lives to someone who hasn't proved His loyalty to our best interests? *Fuhgeddaboudit!*

The writer of Hebrews offers a bit of insight into this aspect of faith: "Now faith is being sure of what we hope for and certain of what we do not see" (11:1). Reason alone says, "You have to see it to believe it," but faith asserts, "You have to believe it to see it." Saint Augustine said it more eloquently: "Understanding is the reward of faith. Therefore do not seek to understand in order to believe, but believe that thou mayest understand."[1]

Faith means being sure that God will come through for you and in fact is already at work on your behalf, even when things seem completely hopeless. At the same time, however, faith doesn't require you to check your brains at the door. The Bible is jam-packed with examples of God's faithfulness, and those who are willing to watch with an open heart and mind will find evidence all around that God has not withdrawn to some distant place but is actively, lovingly at work in our world.

Sincere faith is beautiful, rare, sacred, and intriguing in those who possess it. But it also is sometimes threatening to those whose spiritual eyes are closed. Not everyone is pleased when you seek and draw close to God. You can hear the whispers: *She's getting weird since she found religion. She's off on a tangent, reading the Bible too much, going to prayer meetings. Doesn't she care about having fun anymore?*

To this day, some relatives still refer to me as "a born-again." Every Christmas, one of them inquires, "Hey, are you still a born-again?" to which I lovingly respond, "Yeah, are you still a heathen?" Although my family knows I'm joking with them in love, it's true that faith often transforms us in ways our families and friends may not understand. In truth, we ourselves may not always have a clear understanding of where our faith is leading us. Thankfully, we do know who serves as our trustworthy guide.

Lifestyles of the Rich in Faith

In Hebrews 11, a marvelous chapter on faith, we find a list of those who made the cut for heaven's all-star lineup. One of the most famous inductees into "The Hall of Faith" is Abraham. This biblical patriarch offers a clear example of a life transformed by faith.

In Genesis 12:1–2, we find God speaking to him: "Leave your country, your people and your father's household and go to the land I will show you. I will make you into a great nation and I will bless you; I will make your name great, and you will be a blessing."

Consider what this meant for Abraham. God asked him to leave behind all that was familiar and go…well, the "where" part was a little vague. Hebrews 11:8 tells us that Abraham "obeyed and went, even though he did not know where he was going." He walked in the direction God led, with no map, no points of reference, not even a GPS. He left behind his cozy situation in Haran, where everyone knew him well as the successful son of Terah and grandson of Nahor, and became a travelin' man, an outsider wherever he went. Abraham's faith was based solely on God's word to him and, as Hebrews 11 tells us, his was a "longing for a better country—a heavenly one" (verse 16).

Here was a man willing not only to be transformed but to take steps to make that transformation a reality. Many of us want to change and grow, but we don't want to go! That's why weight-loss pills and supplements are so popular—we want transformation without changing our diets or going to the trouble of exercising. Abraham, however, actively stepped out in faith, trusting God to fulfill the four promises He made in those two brief verses:

1. Property: "Go to the land I will show you" (verse 1).
2. People: "I will make you into a great nation" (verse 2).
3. Prosperity: "I will bless you" (verse 2).
4. Prominence: "I will make your name great, and you will be a blessing" (verse 2).

You may be thinking, *That's all very nice for old Father Abraham, but what on earth do those promises have to do with me?* We're so glad you asked! In Romans 4:13, Paul states that "it was not through law that Abraham and his offspring received the promise…but through the righteousness that comes by faith." *It is not through law* simply means that God doesn't keep His promises just because a person is a good Jew or a religious zealot, or strives to keep the 613 commandments found in the Torah. God makes and keeps His promises to those who have a righteousness that comes by sincere faith in Him.

Scripture declares that through our faith we have been grafted into the house of David, the root of Jesse, the sons of Jacob. In other words, we've been adopted. A friend of Ellie's, who has a terrific relationship with her adoptive parents, likes to say, "Ya can't adopt a baby in the backseat of a car. Adoption is never accidental; it is highly intentional." And she's right! On Good Friday, God intentionally and deliberately took the necessary steps to authorize His only Son to bring us into a grand and vast family. In Galatians 3:14 we read, "He redeemed us in order that the blessing given to Abraham might come to the Gentiles through Christ Jesus." That is great news! We are no longer paupers wandering aimlessly through dark alleys; instead we are daughters of the King, heirs of God, princesses dwelling in a well-lit castle. How great is God to do that for us!

Verse 29 states, "If you belong to Christ, then you are Abraham's seed, and heirs according to the promise." Go ahead, read it again, and then get excited and make some noise and do a little dance. Winning the lottery pales in comparison to the gifts God freely offers to those who love Him.

So let's look again at the four promises God gave to Abraham—and to us, through faith—to see how each leads to a more abundant life.

Faith Transforms the Boundaries of Our Property

Go to the land I will show you. (Genesis 12:1)

In fulfilling His promise to Abraham, God gave his descendants the land of Canaan, a territory extending from the river of Egypt to the river Euphrates (see Genesis 15:18). While much of the land was rocky and mountainous, it also encompassed fertile river valleys and coastal plains. In the years that followed, its location on key trade routes would create many opportunities for those living in the Promised Land.

As heirs of Abraham, God invites us to go with Him to discover the land He wants to give us. Sometimes the land will be a literal place; He may bless you, and others through you, with opportunities in a rehab center, a halfway house, a crisis pregnancy center, a homeless shelter, a senior center, your church, or your own home as you generously welcome people in need of hospitality and grace.

But the land with which God wants to bless us can also refer to the territory within, the space where the Holy Spirit makes His home. "Do you not know that your body is a temple of the Holy Spirit, who is in you, whom you have received from God?" (1 Corinthians 6:19). We all have intangible real estate within our minds and hearts that the Lord desires to occupy, invest in, and use for His glory and our gain.

For example, I (Ellie) have always loved words and wanted to be a teacher for as long as I can remember. As I look back over the years, it's clear that God has continually enlarged my boundaries of influence as I stepped out in faith to claim each opportunity He provided. Teaching children at the local Jewish center led to teaching inner-city kids during summer camp. Teaching a Bible study in my college dorm led to student teaching at a Hispanic school in Boston. Teaching English led to teaching the debate team. Teaching at youth group lock-ins and sleepovers led to teaching young women on campus. Teaching on a radio show led to teaching at a full-day women's conference, and that led to teaching at a three-day retreat, and that led to more than I can ever list here.

Our children, our friends, and our families are also forms of land. God gives us these relationships with the expectation that we will tend them as a dedicated farmer tends a crop, hoping to reap a harvest from her hard work. Jesus used this imagery when He talked about seizing opportunities to share our faith with others. "Do you not say, 'Four months more and then the harvest'? I tell you, open your eyes and look at the fields! They are ripe for harvest" (John 4:35). Survey the land around you, and open your eyes to the potential for harvest in your relationships at home, at the office, in your neighborhood and community.

What places and property does God have in store for you? Say yes when He calls, and you'll be off on an amazing adventure. Remember: to go somewhere, you have to leave somewhere. This could mean moving to a new job, investing in a new ministry, or ending an unhealthy relationship, or it could mean that God is calling you to conquer the geography of memories and emotions so He can expand your boundaries in wholly unexpected ways.

Following where God leads may not require us to literally pack up and move, but when we claim His promises by faith, we inevitably will find ourselves walking in unknown territory. Just as Abraham's descendants were challenged to be strong and courageous as they conquered the land God gave them, so we are to respond boldly whenever and wherever He calls us to take on the responsibilities of ownership, whether at home, in our careers, in ministry, or anywhere else.

Faith Transforms Our Relationships with People

I will make you into a great nation. (Genesis 12:2)

God in effect told Abraham, "I'm going to give you people. You'll be blessed with children. You'll have more descendants than your mind can imagine. Try counting the stars, and if that doesn't paint a clear word picture, head to the seashore and start counting the grains of sand."

Actually, this promise first came when our hero's name was still Abram, which means "exalted father." The irony of bearing that name while remaining childless surely was not lost on him, but imagine the thoughts that coursed through his mind when God later changed his name to Abraham, which means "father of many." A man of lesser faith might have dismissed it as a painful cosmic joke, but Abraham chose to trust God, and his faith was rewarded.

It's nearly impossible to calculate the number of people whose lives have been affected by Abraham's faith. In fact, the genealogy in Matthew 1 traces a direct path from Abraham all the way to Joseph, the adoptive father of Jesus. So Abraham's faith paved the way for ours.

As we've already seen, through faith we have become Abraham's heirs, expanding his family through generation upon generation of believers. And God calls us to pass on the good news of Jesus to those He places in our lives. In other words, God promises to bless us with people. He has gifted us with relationships not to torture us, though with some people it seems that way, but to give us the privilege of carrying His love to others and receiving His love from them. Like Abraham, each of us has the potential to touch more lives than we know as we surrender our interactions to His purposes and let go of our own selfish ideas of relationship.

As mentioned earlier I taught high-school English for ten years. I married the marvelous Frank Lofaro in the middle of my teaching career. Because we were without children during the first five years of our marriage, I was able to do many things with my free time. I coached the cheerleaders in the fall and the volleyball team in the winter. I advised the Interact Rotary Club and the debate team. In 1984, Congress passed the Equal Access Act, and I became the advisor of the school's first Christian club. I participated in faculty-student competitions and spent many late-afternoon and dinner hours listening to kids' stories of frustrated love lives, splintered friendships, and abusive parents. I did my very best to dispense wise counsel and direction, but more than advice, most kids were immensely grateful for an ear and a hug.

In retrospect, I learned far more than I taught during those colorful years, and I was blessed beyond calculation by the people God brought my way. Then after a decade in the classroom, I chose to become a domestic engineer. I stayed home and produced three bona fide Italian babies within five years. No pay, hard work, long hours, periodic grief—and immeasurable gratification. Those little people have now grown into big people and continue to bless my life in infinite ways.

God wants to bless you with people to touch, know, impact, forgive, evangelize, be kind to, guide. Are you prepared to receive them into your life? Who are the people that God wants you to meet, reach, help, care for, and impact? Who are the people you already know but who know nothing about your faith? What influence is God calling you to have in the lives of those in the next room, next door, in the next office, or on the next bench in the park?

God has promised you people to love and to be loved by. Are you taking Him up on His promise?

Faith Transforms Our Prospects of Prosperity

I will bless you. (Genesis 12:2)

Abraham enjoyed numerous blessings, including professional and financial success as a wealthy rancher. God's blessings of prosperity extended down through his descendants as well: from Joseph's divinely inspired provision against the threat of famine, through the New Testament account of Jesus's multiplying the loaves and fishes for a hungry crowd, God fulfilled His promise to more than meet the needs of Abraham's children.

And as Abraham's offspring through faith, we have access to unimaginable prosperity as well. I am not speaking about our shallow American version of this word, although I do believe God wants to bless us with food and shelter. We are not going to be effective for the kingdom if we are constantly hiding from bill collectors. More than anything, however, this prosperity has to do with life's intangibles. In God's economy, prosperity is not so much about dollars and cents as it is about spiritual riches. That's what Paul was referring to when he wrote, "I pray also that the eyes of your heart may be enlightened in order that you may know the hope to which he has called you, the riches of his glorious inheritance in the saints" (Ephesians 1:18).

True prosperity—all the riches of God's grace—is available to anyone who can make this declaration:

> I am a Christian. I believe with all my heart, mind, and soul that Jesus Christ came to earth to save and secure the future of the human race. I believe that His teachings were accurately recorded in the gospels and that His story is told from Genesis to Revelation. The Bible is my manual for living. God made me, so when I need to be tuned up, cleaned up, or lifted up, I return to the Maker of my soul. He knows me fully and loves me completely. That's *rare*. He has a plan for my life but offers me free will to

choose as I please. That's *respect*. He sent His only Son to pay my spiritual debt and has personally promised that I will live forever. That's *remarkable*. He is my guide and has never let me go or led me astray. He will bring me home safely. That's incredibly *reassuring*.

What greater prosperity could we want? The Bible contradicts the world's idea of wealth, saying, "But godliness with contentment is great gain. For we brought nothing into the world, and we can take nothing out of it. But if we have food and clothing, we will be content with that" (1 Timothy 6:6–8). Contentment, peace, gratitude—all of these compose spiritual richness. A prosperous heart is a grateful one and doesn't pine for what it doesn't have. It accepts that we can't have all our wants and believes that God lovingly withholds some of them so He can meet our greater needs instead.

Gaining this kind of perspective and wisdom is essential to prospering. Yet so often we slip into a spirit of ungratefulness. First we want to see what we get, and then we'll decide if we need to be thankful.

By contrast, Philippians 4:6 reminds us to present our requests to God *with thanksgiving*. The Bible teaches us to thank God in advance of what He is going to do. In this way, thankfulness is an exercise of faith, believing what we don't yet see. Jesus left the wealth of heaven in order to don a robe and sandals, but He continued to give thanks at all times. He publicly thanked the Father in advance for what He would do through many miracles. He thanked God for hearing His prayer even before He called Lazarus from the grave. At the Last Supper with His disciples, He gave thanks for the simple meal of bread and drink.

Want to discover just how wealthy you are, how God is fulfilling His promise to bless you? Take inventory of all you have, and begin developing a thankful heart.

Faith Transforms Our Definition of Prominence

I will make your name great, and you will be a blessing. (Genesis 12:2)

God promised not only to give Abraham property, people, and prosperity but also to make his name great. Without a doubt, this promise has been fulfilled, since Jews, Christians, and Muslims all revere him as the father of their faiths.

While it's unlikely that any of us will attain Abraham's level of name recognition, as children of the promise, we wield enormous levels of influence when, in faith, we fulfill the roles to which God calls us.

Let's consider for a moment the Proverbs 31 woman, the one we love to hate because she highlights all our insecurities. And yet when you get right down to it, every verse about her simply reveals a woman who completes even the most mundane tasks faithfully and cheerfully. The result? "Her children arise and call her blessed; her husband also, and he praises her.... Give her the reward she has earned, and let her works bring her praise at the city gate" (verses 28, 31). That's the kind of greatness any of us can achieve; it simply means refusing to settle for less than what God has gifted us to be.

We gain prominence when, along with Abraham, we claim God's promise: "You will be a blessing." Of course, because we are jaded Brooklyn natives, phrases like, "You're such a blessing," don't flow naturally from our lips. We'd be more apt to say, "You're the best!" or, "Who's better than you?" Who among us doesn't thrive on such words of praise? But they mean the most when they come from God, and He wants to raise us to prominence in those specific areas where He has gifted us.

None of us will be good at everything. For example, I (Ellie) am not particularly gifted in the domestic arts. When I scream, "Dinner!" my children run to the car. But those things that I can do well, I want to do extremely well. And even the things I don't do well, I want to do with all my heart, remembering that I'm ultimately working for the Lord (see Colossians 3:23). I don't want to be a mediocre woman; I want to be great. For my glory? No, for God's.

Gaining prominence isn't about making a name for ourselves but about allowing God to magnify His name through us. When committed believers excel at whatever it is they do, the praise ultimately goes to God. He receives the praise, honor, and glory He is fully worthy to receive.

Remember, many of our biblical heroes logged countless hours in the unglamorous role of shepherd. When you're feeling unappreciated at home, picture the future King David with his herd of sheep: leading the stubborn critters to food, preparing a safe place for them to lie down, getting them yet another drink when he'd rather be composing a psalm. You get the picture.

God loves us uniquely and has designed for us a destiny laced with blessing; it's our job to move toward it in faith, one step at a time.

What do you do, and how do you do it? Are you involved with scrapbooking? Be creative with it. Do you work as an accountant? Be amazingly accurate. Are you a mother changing diapers all day? Do it cheerfully. It is highly rewarding to complete a big project or a menial task and to do the job well and with devotion and integrity. Whether it's accounting, laying bricks, baking a cake, or running a company—whatever it is you're doing at this stage of life—be great at it, and God will bless your reputation. He will "make your name great" how and when He wants.

Take a Leap of Faith

When we entrust ourselves to God, His promises, and His purposes, we embark on an exciting adventure, joining those men and women featured in God's Hall of Faith—people like Abraham, Joseph, Moses, David, and Rahab—who placed their faith in a God who cares about the details of our lives. When we truly believe this, we'll find our days transformed by a sense of anticipation about what God is doing and how we can play a part.

I (Kathy) woke up one morning feeling a strong conviction that I was to send three hundred dollars to my sister Jennifer. Along with that nudge from God came the firm impression that I was to instruct her to spend it on clothes. How controlling! I'd had the privilege of surprising my sister with random gifts before, but I had never attached a requirement about what to do with any money I gave her. It felt so awkward.

Am I hearing You right, Lord? Still He gently pressed upon me to have that conversation with her. So I did. The words had barely left my lips when my sister started to cry. "Kath, I woke up this morning and told the Lord that I felt like I was being selfish with my prayer, with all the needs in this world. But I asked Him if He would provide for me so that I would be able to get some new summer clothes. I have been wearing the same things for three summers in a row. I dreaded getting them out of the attic again." As my eyes filled to the brim at her words, I thought, *You are amazingly intimate, Jesus.* Such a small request. But how like our God, who hears and cares about every prayer from a heart reaching out with faith—and who uses those of us who listen carefully for His voice and choose to respond in faith.

The walk of faith is an exciting adventure. "No eye has seen, no ear has heard, no mind has conceived what God has prepared for those who love Him" (1 Corinthians 2:9). God has so much in store for us that we cannot begin to imagine it all. Great things await. Faith truly does transform!

Thoughts to *Noodle* On

1. In what ways have you fallen into the all-too-common trap of "do everything, have everything, be everything"?

2. What would shift in your priorities if you were living with an awareness of God's active involvement in your life?

3. Describe one way in which God's promise of prominence can be clearly seen in your life.

4. What one thing can you do today to be a blessing to someone whom God has positioned you to influence?

Chapter 2

Faith That Triumphs

When your eyes are on the goal,
no obstacle can hold you back

My (Ellie's) paternal extended family is loud, proud, and patriotic about two countries. Theirs is the classic immigrant story, shared by two million Italians, of crossing the Atlantic to New York Harbor in the early nineteen hundreds. My dad's parents arrived in "Merica" with true grit, big dreams, high hopes, and a suitcase.

Though their Brooklyn neighborhood was not exactly lined with gold, it offered a safe haven and held great promise for the education and advancement of their eleven children, who would never know the backbreaking agricultural life of Calabria, Italy.

Until he and his six younger siblings were reunited on American soil, Papa Mannarino regularly sent to southern Italy a portion of his earnings from making cane chairs and delivering ice blocks. He held various other jobs as well, and fifteen years after signing the immigrant roster at Ellis Island, he opened a small luncheonette that sold sandwiches, shakes, and cigars. His American dream had come true.

His son, my dad, carried on that noble work ethic as he studied insurance at night, worked various jobs by day, and drove a hearse every weekend so he and Mom could afford to leave Brooklyn and raise their five kids on a small lot of land with a new split-level home, fresh air, and dozens of kids on the same block. When he turned forty, Dad moved us to a wooded acre with a pool and a spacious colonial. He left a secure career with Allstate and proudly opened the Mannarino Insurance Agency. It was another dream come true.

My father's family had no patience for whining; they were interested in winning. Whether at a stickball game, a card game, or a Yankees game, their competitive spirits battled at full tilt. They entered into every experience of life with passion and a determination to overcome any obstacle.

As I think back on their enthusiasm for life, I can't help but wonder why more of us don't live that way. When you wake up in the morning, is the first thought in your mind more likely to be a joyful, "Good morning, Lord!" or a begrudging, "Good Lord, it's morning"?

Mama Mannarino's Meatballs

The world's best meatballs, to be enjoyed right out of the frying pan or the fridge.

Ingredients

- 1 pound ground meat (most stores offer a meatloaf combo of beef, veal, and pork)
- 2 tablespoons chopped parsley
- 1/4 teaspoon garlic powder
- 1/4 teaspoon pepper
- 1/4 teaspoon salt
- 2 eggs
- 1 cup grated cheese
- 1 cup dry breadcrumbs
- olive oil to coat skillet

Our choice to feast daily on abundant faith makes all the difference in our outlook on life. When we take note of and celebrate that "this is the day the LORD has made; let us rejoice and be glad in it" (Psalm 118:24), why would we want to linger in bed and hide away from the world? Transforming faith enables us to overcome our circumstances rather than be overwhelmed by them. When we fully grasp our rightful inheritance in God's family, we stop seeing ourselves as victims and instead live as victors. We move from being people with complaints to being people with testimonies.

This does not mean that the life of faith is void of trouble. Take a look at our forefathers and foremothers in Scripture; they had plenty of heartaches and sorrows. We rejoice with you if this is a sweet, trouble-free season in your life, but for all of us, difficulties and sorrows will come. Hardships are a reality of life on earth. The good news is that we do not need to be derailed or destroyed by sad news, financial deficits, broken relationships, poor health, or natural disasters.

Cooking Instructions

1. Blend all ingredients except olive oil in a bowl. Portion the ground meat into the meatball size you prefer (we use an ice-cream scoop!), then roll firmly and rapidly in your palms. Set aside on counter or plate.
2. Coat skillet with olive oil; heat. When oil is hot, place meatballs in it. Reduce heat to medium and cook 3 to 5 minutes. Then turn meatballs over and cook another few minutes. Leave a few in longer—some people like them very browned.

Note: This recipe can be doubled or tripled, since half of the meatballs will be eaten before the meal. Of what remains, drop some in meat sauce and save the rest for warm hoagies, smothered with melted cheese.

The person of faith responds *differently* to life's difficulties. We will surely have trials, but God desires to turn each trial into a triumph.

The Thrill of Victory

Triumph is a powerful word, isn't it? It encompasses the ideas of victory, success, exaltation, winning! The impassioned apostle Paul thought a good deal about winning. Several times in his New Testament writings, he refers to the race of life and how we are supposed to keep moving, stick it out, and finish the course set before us.

> I consider my life worth nothing to me, if only I may finish the race and complete the task the Lord Jesus has given me—the task of testifying to the gospel of God's grace. (Acts 20:24)

> Do you not know that in a race all the runners run, but only one gets the prize? Run in such a way as to get the prize. (1 Corinthians 9:24)

Triumph also implies a contest or struggle. For me (Ellie) it conjures images of the Olympic Games and childhood memories of watching *Wide World of Sports* with my dad and three brothers. I can still hear Jim McKay's voice harkening, "The thrill of victory—and the agony of defeat!" That program came on the air when I was five years old, and I still vividly recall powerfully charged images of athletes experiencing the gamut of emotions from extreme jubilation to deep grief and unbearable physical pain. I still wince when I think of the ski jumper wiping out and tumbling down the mountain like a runaway snowball.

In the life of faith, just as in sports, victory comes only when we rise to a challenge, when we strive to gain the upper hand against whatever or whoever threatens to hold us back. The author of Hebrews wrote about this as well:

> Therefore, since we are surrounded by such a great cloud of witnesses, let us throw off everything that hinders and the sin that so easily entangles, and let us run with perseverance the race marked out for us. (12:1)

Have you found your faith hindered by the distractions of life? An unexpected diagnosis, a police officer at the door, a car that needs repair, a child in a failure cycle at school, a rift with a family member. When we find ourselves up against such difficulties, our choices are *fight* or *flight*. When we're living by faith, we'll always choose the first option. We need not give in to fear and faithlessness, because we know that the Lord will never abandon us.

Let's look at how The Message translates Paul's description of living with triumphant faith:

> I'm not saying that I have this all together, that I have it made. But I am
> well on my way, reaching out for Christ, who has so wondrously reached
> out for me. Friends, don't get me wrong: By no means do I count myself
> an expert in all of this, but I've got my eye on the goal, where God is beck-
> oning us onward—to Jesus. I'm off and running, and I'm not turning back.
> (Philippians 3:12–14)

The triumphant faith Paul describes is not a cocky "I'm right, you're doomed" sort of faith but a faith fully invested in living life to the fullest. Triumphant faith is energized by a certainty of purpose that propels us forward no matter what obstacles litter our path.

The Agony of Defeat

Sadly, not enough of us exercise triumphant faith on a daily basis. What happens when we take our eyes off the goal, when we forget what it is we're ultimately striving for—becoming like Jesus—and when we instead focus on circumstances? We quickly get ground under the wheels of temptation, discouragement, or weariness.

The biblical character Jehoshaphat illustrates how this happens. You can read about this great-great-grandson of Solomon in 2 Chronicles 17–20 as well as 1 Kings 15 and 22.

Now, in a sort of roundabout way, Jehoshaphat reminds me (Ellie) a bit of myself. Anyway, Jehoshaphat—let's call him JJ, short for *Jehoshaphat of Judah*— exhibited a faith that was triumphant on many levels:

- JJ was a bold follower of God. "His heart was devoted to the ways of the LORD" (2 Chronicles 17:6).

  Hey, so am I!

- He carried out a national program of religious education. "In the third year of his reign he sent his officials…to teach in the towns of Judah.… They taught throughout Judah, taking with them the Book of the Law of the LORD; they went around to all the towns of Judah and taught the people" (2 Chronicles 17:7, 9).

  Me too! I travel coast to coast and teach whoever will listen.

- He developed an extensive legal structure throughout the kingdom. "He appointed judges in the land, in each of the fortified cities of Judah.… In Jerusalem also, Jehoshaphat appointed some of the Levites, priests and heads of Israelite families to administer the law of the LORD and to settle disputes" (2 Chronicles 19:5, 8).

  Well, I've created and enforced tons of laws for my three little minions, and I've settled more disputes than a Little League umpire.

- He found the fear of God to be a key motivator for those within his influence. "The fear of the LORD fell on all the kingdoms of the lands surrounding Judah, so that they did not make war with Jehoshaphat" (2 Chronicles 17:10).

  Those little minions became large teenagers—'nuf said.

Sadly, the similarities don't end there. Jehoshaphat also dealt with unfortunate consequences from poor choices and personal failures:

- He did not completely destroy idolatry in the land.

  Where's the harm in a little chocolate worship?

- He became entangled in ungodly alliances.

  I have looked for acceptance from people rather than God.

- He failed to anticipate the long-term results of his decisions.

  Umm. Well.

- He did not listen to the voice of God's messenger.

  . . . .

Can you see me squirm? Can you feel my pain? *Oooch, ouch,* and *eeech.* I'm guilty on all four counts.

Let's look a bit more closely at where it all went wrong for this promising young king and see if you, like me, recognize yourself in any of his mistakes.

Dangerous Liaisons

In 2 Chronicles 17, we read that JJ succeeded his father Asa as king of Judah. Things were looking good for the kingdom because here was a man who knew the power of faith: "The LORD was with Jehoshaphat because in his early years he walked in the ways his father David had followed" (verse 3).

But all too soon he was seduced by power, position, and possessions. To make matters worse, he entered into business ventures and battle plans that were not of God's leading. Along the way he formed an alliance with the ungodly King Ahab of Israel by allowing his son to marry Ahab's daughter.

Ahab is the poster child for the maxim "Bad company corrupts good character" (1 Corinthians 15:33). When we allow ourselves to be taken in by people who aren't motivated by genuine love, we soon learn to our sorrow that the world is full of false friends and lovers who bribe and entice with empty promises, seductive arrangements, and shallow self-seeking relationships. They appear to care, but in truth they're concerned only with their own gain. They are users, and as JJ learned, putting your faith in such people rather than relying solely on the all-faithful God can lead to being run over by temptation and trouble.

Willful Disregard for the Truth

When King Ahab asked JJ to join with him in an attack on Ramoth Gilead, the godly young king felt a bit uneasy, even though all of Ahab's prophets urged them to go for it. He wanted to be sure God was on their side. In response to JJ's inquiries, Ahab finally brought forward a prophet known for telling the truth, no matter how ugly. This man, Micaiah, contradicted popular opinion by predicting a terrible defeat for Ahab and JJ (see 2 Chronicles 18).

Micaiah embodied what trustworthy friends are all about. They tell the truth when the truth is unpopular. They know God's voice, and they share His mandates even if it upsets everyone else in the room. Their allegiance doesn't change with the weather. You should count yourself rich and deeply blessed if you have one or two Micaiahs who care about you.

Years ago I (Kathy) fell fast and hard for a man who was not in love with me. But in that state of heart you can't imagine that the other person doesn't feel the same way. Ours was a long-distance relationship, and I spent more time than I care to admit waiting for his phone calls or some suggestion as to when we might see each other next. It was so unlike me, because I am usually in the driver's seat when it comes to romantic relationships. This time my heart was moving full speed ahead with someone else at the wheel.

Over time he became distant and slightly rude. Rather than taking the hint, I decided to fly to where he was and reason with him. Surely this could be worked out. *Maybe if he lays eyes on me one more time, he'll wake up to what he's in danger of losing!* Boy, did I have to buffer my self-esteem.

Then my doorbell rang, and Ellie was at the door. She came into my living room and sat me down. Our conversation went something like this:

"What are you doing?"

"What do you mean, what am I doing?"

"Kath, listen. He does not love you."

"But…"

"He does not love you."

I cried and cried, but I knew she was speaking the truth. God had been trying to get my attention, but I kept running ahead of Him. When we want something bad enough, we tend to block out God's voice saying no. Thank God Ellie told me what she knew I *needed* to hear.

Ahab, unfortunately, preferred prophets who told him what he *wanted* to hear, so he had Micaiah imprisoned and given only bread and water. Still, Micaiah never budged, and he warned the kings once again that they would not return safely. "Mark my words" (2 Chronicles 18:27). Ahab and Jehoshaphat chose to ignore his warning, and here's what happened: in the middle of the battle, "someone drew his bow at random and hit the king of Israel between the sections of his armor.… At sunset [Ahab] died" (verses 33–34). Micaiah's prophecy of doom had come to pass.

Seeking God and then ignoring His instruction does not lead to victorious living. I (Ellie) can personally attest to that. Like JJ, I have sometimes outwardly sought the Lord but then chosen to make a few adjustments to His perfect plan, especially when it involves detours and discipline. I want to enjoy God's blessings, yet I do not always respond wisely or well when He asks me to set aside my desires in order to run the race He has called me to. When the voice of God causes discomfort and possibly insult, we may be tempted to have our Micaiah's voice shut out, starved, and silenced from our self-directed agendas.

But as JJ discovered, just because we cover our ears doesn't mean God has stopped speaking. "When Jehoshaphat king of Judah returned safely to his palace in Jerusalem, Jehu the seer, the son of Hanani, went out to meet him and said to the king, 'Should you help the wicked and love those who hate the LORD? Because of this, the wrath of the LORD is upon you' " (2 Chronicles 19:1–2).

Imagine how Jehoshaphat felt; his friend Ahab was dead, and he himself was on the receiving end of some divine anger. Might have been time to rethink his priorities, wouldn't you agree? And maybe it's time for us to do the same.

The God of Great Comebacks

As JJ so effectively demonstrates, taking our eyes off the Lord is a prescription for defeat. But, thankfully, even when we get turned around and lost on our journey of faith, He doesn't give up on us. He's out there cheering us on, waving His arms to get our attention and redirect our gaze toward the finish line.

Skipping ahead to 2 Chronicles 20, we find JJ receiving news that a huge army was about to pounce on him. Needless to say, he was a nervous wreck, which is where we get the expression, "Jumpin' Jehoshaphat!" (Ellie's *personal* explanation; please don't write to us on this.) But God was right there, waiting for JJ to readjust his focus so He could turn this trial into triumph.

In his darkest moment, with a tsunami of manpower, knives, and swords about to crash over him, Jehoshaphat did what he'd been taught to do as a young child: he prayed. He trusted God and worshiped Him. The king called for a national time of fasting. And then he prayed some more. He acknowledged God's power, might, and goodness. He praised God and gave thanks in the middle of his trial—before the answer came. We would do well to emulate him.

God then declared through the prophet Jahaziel:

Do not be afraid or discouraged because of this vast army. For the battle is not yours, but God's.... You will not have to fight this battle. Take up your positions; stand firm and see the deliverance the LORD will give you.... Do not be afraid; do not be discouraged. Go out to face them tomorrow, and the LORD will be with you. (verses 15, 17)

Wow. Quite an impressive promise from the great I AM.

With this encouragement to propel him forward, JJ assembled his people and appointed a group of men to lead the army into battle while singing to God and praising Him for the splendor of His holiness. They went forth to fight, singing, "Give thanks to the LORD, for his love endures forever" (verse 21). And the Lord gave them an incredible victory over their enemies.

The same God who delivered JJ is the God who created us, knows us, protects us, guides us, loves us, and desires to have intimacy with us. He is the God who always was and is and always will be. We can try to play hide-and-seek with Him, but He is still there, and He sees all. We can disobey Him, but He is willing to forgive and to come to our rescue. We can ignore His will, but if we are truly contrite and turn to Him in faith, He will deliver us from our troubles to a place of triumphant rejoicing. The battle is *His*.

Training for the Championship

JJ's story shows that triumphant faith comes only when we elude the snarls of temptation, when we toss aside the distractions and fears that hinder us and when we grab hold of God for all we're worth. We're not saying the life of faith is easy. In fact, Scripture urges us to "contend earnestly for the faith" (Jude 3, NASB).

Now while Mr. Webster informs us that *contend* means "to fight, to compete, to assert, to struggle," the Greek meaning of *to contend* is more literally "to agonize," as an athlete achieving victory by meeting or exceeding his or her personal best.

Have you agonized in order to see certain results in your life? Are you prepared to withstand the full press of the Adversary?

Every day brings many opportunities for us to contend, fight, and agonize for our faith. We can make conscious efforts to keep our tempers in the midst of family squabbles, to remain calm when we're cut off in traffic, to hold our tongues when "Miss Perfect" at church makes a comment about our wriggly children, and to trust God to defend us from gossip. Maybe we can do better at turning off certain television programs, avoiding certain magazines, and responding with kindness to the not-so-nice neighbor. In whatever situations arise, we can strive to achieve our personal best for our own well-being and for the cause of Christ.

We must earnestly contend against temptation and trials with a victorious faith that is confident in God's sovereignty and His ability to deliver us safely to the next shore. In the gospel of Mark we read that Jesus tells us to have faith in God, to speak words of faith, and to pray in faith, trusting that God will answer (see 11:22–24). We are to protect our hearts and minds against unbelief. "Be on guard. Stand firm in the faith. Be courageous. Be strong" (1 Corinthians 16:13, NLT).

Fighting the Good Fight

I (Ellie) have had the immense privilege of speaking at several national conferences at Willow Creek Community Church in Illinois. At one particular event I was wowed by a dynamic young pastor named Dr. David A. Anderson, who shared a message titled "How to Have a Good Fight." He described how Paul of Tarsus loved young Timothy like a son. As you know, every good dad teaches his son how to handle himself: how to navigate a course, a track, a maze, or a mountain, and yes, even how to handle a bully.

In this vein, Paul speaks of the "good fight" three separate times:

Timothy, my son, I give you this instruction in keeping with the prophecies once made about you, so that by following them you may fight the good fight. (1 Timothy 1:18)

Fight the good fight of the faith. Take hold of the eternal life to which you were called when you made your good confession in the presence of many witnesses. (1 Timothy 6:12)

I have fought the good fight, I have finished the race, I have kept the faith. (2 Timothy 4:7)

You may wonder if all this talk of fighting applies to nice Christian women like us, but let me tell you, growing up with three brothers, I learned at a young age how to block a sucker punch and inflict a half nelson. Those are great visuals for how even the most "delicate" among us can deal with the temptations and trials of life.

Going the Distance

Faith is often referred to as a muscle, because it must be used often and given proper attention for optimal results. James 1:3 tells us that "the testing of [our] faith develops perseverance." That is what faith can do for you! Oh, how we need perseverance in this race called life if we're to press on and finish well. Whether you're striving in the workplace, mentoring the less fortunate, raising children, impacting communities, caring for a loved one with Alzheimer's, or even trying to lose ten pounds—perseverance in pursuit of victory is absolutely vital.

Let's Dish About...
Everyday Challenges to Faith

KT: Ellie, do you sometimes find it relatively easy to have faith for the big problems but completely lose perspective over the little things?

EL: Absolutely! I seem to have weathered difficult things fairly well while maintaining an eternal perspective. The loss of a close friend to cancer while in college, my parents' divorce, the six-inch accidental cut into my bladder during an emergency C-section to deliver Paris, the WWII-style incision across my private parts to deliver Jordan (Capri was easy), the removal of some skin cancer from my shin, my broken back, my dad's death, the shock and aftermath of 9/11. I can honestly say that I faced and processed all of these personal trials with faith, hope, and supernatural peace.

However, my responses tend to be a bit less holy when I'm up against

The reality is, we will always face opposition. Life is much more of a crawl through the land mines than a tiptoe through the tulips. The encouraging news is, we can persevere with faith in the midst of opposition, resistance, and daunting hurdles because we know that God never looks away and is always right on time.

There is an awful lot of waiting in the Bible. The falsely accused Joseph (see Genesis 37–50) comes to mind when we think of perseverance in faith. He continued to believe in God's active involvement in his life, even when he had every reason to give up. Rather than viewing himself as a victim of mistreatment, betrayal, and abandonment, he did things with such excellence that he continued to be promoted. The ultimate triumph of being appointed governor of Egypt did not negate Joseph's seventeen long years of unjust treatment, but it certainly spoke loudly of

things like delayed carpools, closet cleaning, attempting to produce the four food groups all at once, getting to the post office, the vet, and the orthodontist on time, and finding a leak from the kids' tub coming through the foyer ceiling just before dinner guests arrive. Let's just say that I will *never* invite cameras into my house or my car to tape a reality TV series.

KT: I know what you mean! When the big problems arrive at my door, I feel so desperate that I immediately go to God in prayer. It's the mundane that trips me up. Sometimes I find that the hours get so jam-packed with "stuff" that my awareness of God is crowded out. When little annoyances and problems creep up throughout the day, I tend to grow agitated and bothered, and I start losing my way. But when I deliberately talk with God throughout my everyday moments rather than just in the big events, I am much more at peace and able to deal with things from His perspective.

what a powerful witness he was to all who encountered him. Joseph's determination to forgive his brothers and honor his masters brought blessing and honor to God and saved countless lives. Despite much pain and loss, Joseph was a true winner because he faithfully executed each role and task God placed before him.

> *Chi la dura la vince.*
> **He who perseveres wins at last.**

After more than three decades of running my own race and "fighting the good fight," I (Ellie) feel myself becoming a bit more weary with each lap around the track and each round in the ring. It would give me immense pleasure to lie down on an overstuffed couch for an entire month. I could contemplate the great thinkers, catch up on wonderful books, listen to my favorite music, glance through magazines, and watch the weather change outside my windows. The thought of a season void of deadlines, to-do lists, responsibilities, and repetitive, mindless tasks is quite appealing. Then I return to my senses. (Have you ever seen a person who has voluntarily spent a month on a couch? It's *not* pretty!)

Truth be told, I do not aspire to be a couch potato, nor do I wish to be a bench (or a pew) warmer. I will not settle for being a spectator or a critic or a naysayer. I want to be in the game, and if I can't, I want to be a cheerleader. I want to sing and dance and march and step up to the plate. I want to carpe diem for all I'm worth. I want to climb every mountain and ford every stream. (Can you hear the violins?) I want to go the distance and come out a winner.

Pushing Through the Pain

Everyone loves a winner and everyone loves to *be* a winner. We want our favorite sports teams to win. We want our kids to win in school. We want to win at work and be winsome in relationships. We want to win the Bake-Off and the Monopoly tournament. We hope to win the free weekend getaway, and we wouldn't mind winning that new car. We all aspire to be associated with success.

However, one of the most vital truths about triumphant faith is that what looks like winning to God doesn't always look like winning to us. Consider the events of Good Friday: Jesus was accused, abused, reviled, and then crucified. The Messiah's lifeless body was placed in a tomb. His followers were left devastated by this tragic turn of events. By every human measure, this was failure.

But behind the scenes God was smiling. He knew that His Son had triumphed over sin and would soon triumph over the grave. He knew that these events would lead to the ultimate success: righteousness for everyone who chooses to accept the gift of salvation that His Son's death made available.

In much the same way, the difficulties of life may convince us that we're losing when, in God's eyes, we've already won. He knows the ending of each story, and He knows that suffering leads to perseverance, which leads to character, which leads to hope (see Romans 5:3–4). We'll look more at hope in the chapters to come, but for now just keep in mind that hope and faith are intertwined, like a plate of tangled spaghetti. Together, they feed our souls and strengthen us for whatever life sends our way.

I (Ellie) recently received some personal coaching in what it means to push through the pain and emerge stronger for it. In the early summer of 2005, Frank and I traveled to Florida for what was supposed to be a romantic weekend to celebrate his fiftieth birthday. Though the trip had been planned for months, by the time we landed on Friday afternoon, it was apparent that we would spend the next few days with my dad, who was in hospice care. His left leg had been amputated, he was on kidney dialysis, and he was losing his battle with diabetes. Then there was yet another visit to another hospital on Sunday night to see my dear aunt Ida, who was soon to be ninety years old.

On Monday morning I woke up and declared to Frank that we would redeem the time and have a sweet afternoon before flying home to the kids. I convinced him to rent a motorboat and ride along the Intercoastal Waterway for some lunch. One hour into the pleasant boat ride, a loud and large boat came speeding toward us and created a high wave that crashed into our little seventeen-foot pleasure craft. In a seated position with my legs stretched out, I went up two feet and came down with a force that broke my back in two places. My L5 disc was shattered, and my L1 was fractured. (Captain Frank was unscathed.)

By Monday at noon, after a dramatic EMT and fire-truck rescue, I found myself stretched out in yet *another* hospital, on a morphine drip. I was sporting a white gown with blue dots just like Dad and Aunt Ida had worn. (Now I under-stand why a witty eighty-two-year-old friend of mine refuses to move to Florida; she claims that it is God's waiting room.)

In my pain-filled condition, I remember asking a few questions: *Why me, Lord? Don't you love me? Don't you see me? Couldn't you have calmed that wave? Couldn't you have raptured me before my bottom hit bottom? I have been so busy serving you, and now I have the summer completely off from speaking and writing and I was going to spend quality time with my kids and my husband, but now I'm in a full-body brace! Why, why, why? I think I'm gonna die!*

I convinced Frank to fly home that night to be with the kids. The minutes and hours passed in slow motion. Two days later, I felt an overwhelming urge to get out of there and return to the DC area; maybe it was the weatherman announc-ing that hurricane season would begin the next day. Maybe it was the torrential rain and wind outside my hospital-room window, or maybe it was the minute-long brownout, but it seemed like time to say buh-bye. Kicking into New York mode, I sat up in bed, "gently" demanded a torso brace, asked for an administrator, called United Airlines, requested a wheelchair to get to the front curb, hailed a taxi, and was on my way.

Upon arrival at the West Palm Beach Airport, I was placed back in a wheel-chair, rolled down the Jetway, and helped onto the four o'clock flight. I took just a few baby steps and lowered myself into aisle seat 1C. The flight was full (aren't they all?), and I was grateful to have a seat. I remember uttering an anxious prayer, asking the Lord to extend the positive effects of the pain medication. As I turned my head a bit to the left, I noticed a beautiful but seemingly tired woman in 1A, gazing out her window.

I then took note of her severely disabled teenaged son in 1B. Because of an uncontrollable drooling condition, a small towel had been fashioned into a bib and placed around his neck. I promptly looked away, feeling vulnerable that the boy's spastic flailing might reach in my direction. After takeoff, my spirit settled, and I looked back at that mom who was *still* gazing out the small window. Now I am not one who has heard God speak audibly, but He often makes uniquely deep impressions on my heart and in my thoughts. I "heard" Him quite clearly: *Ellie, this woman is looking into the sky for a brief respite. On most days, her son is all she sees. For the next two hours, you will look at and interact with her son. I will not heal this boy until heaven, but your spine will be healed here on earth. Be very careful about how you define suffering. My ways are not yours. I am the Lord.*

I took a deep breath, thanked the Lord for His comfort, and promised Him (and myself) that I would make every effort to avoid a "Why me?" mentality about life. As many courageous people have said about their illnesses and tragedies, "Why *not* me?"

The time I spent with that young boy on the flight home often came to mind in the days, weeks, and months following my accident, particularly when I had trouble making sense of my pain and the drastic impact on my mobility and, hence, my life. I remained in a body brace for four months, used a walker and a cane, and endured extensive physical therapy for many more weeks. Thankfully, I was able to avoid surgery and any permanent paralysis.

Fast-forward three years, and I am grateful to report that I have shown marked improvement. And I can readily offer several ways I was "blessed" by the accident, though I'll mention only a few.

First of all, I am now literally *drawn* to people in wheelchairs, special braces, and walkers, and as a result I've met many incredible people. I go out of my way to greet these special ones and ask how they are doing. I've learned that people struggling in public settings appreciate not only a helping hand but also a warm greeting. Because I heard some pretty strange remarks and received many stares while wearing that brace, I am much quicker to remember that a physical disability does not equal a mental disability. Two weeks after the accident, on the way home from my dad's funeral, I was at LaGuardia Airport in full regalia: body brace, wheelchair, and cane. Though I was in his view and earshot, the gate agent spoke to Frank about me as if I were brain dead. I wanted to kick him (my legs worked fine), but I thought it would be a poor witness for the kingdom—and for my three teenagers, who were very intentionally staying ten feet behind me.

Another huge blessing came from "the blondes." For all my griping about the unfriendly and formal tone of so many I've encountered in northern Virginia, we were blessed to receive wonderful dinners every night for three months. But I must admit it hurt my feelings a bit when my son Jordan gleefully exclaimed one night at the table, "Mom, you should have broken your back a lot sooner. These meals are great!" Humble yourself in the sight of the Lord—or your kids will do it for you.

The greatest blessing is that my faith grew deeper as I watched God slowly but surely heal my body, though I would like to think that I would still be growing in faith and praising God had my story ended differently.

During those often-sleepless nights lying in that body brace, I thought a great deal about two women whose accidents left them as quadriplegics. Joni Eareckson Tada and Renée Bondi are two mighty heroines of mine. Joni hit her head diving into a lake, and Renée hit her head falling out of bed during a bad dream. Joni's faith could have taken a fatal dive, and Renée's fall could have been just the beginning of a lifelong nightmare. However, these two women defied all odds, and both have found purpose, meaning, and deep joy in the midst of their ongoing trials. I have heard Joni say that when she gets to heaven, she will stand up, grab her wheelchair from behind, swing it around with her right arm, hand it over to God, and say, "Thanks, Lord, I needed that." I have listened intently as Renée described a conversation with God in which she, too, felt compelled to thank Him for her wheelchair. That is the faith that lifts our eyes toward heaven. That is the faith that triumphs over circumstances.

You may have been through much deeper pain than mine, and your whys may seem to be more valid. You may be unable to see blessings in the midst of your trouble. But let's remember that not everything is clear in this sometimes dim and dark world. As the apostle Paul reminds us, assessing life on planet earth is like staring into a flea-market mirror (see 1 Corinthians 13:12). The mirror is in decent condition, but the silver is chipping at the edges and the cloudy glass offers a darkened, hazy reflection. One day, however, we will see clearly and understand all things.

The mystery of faith is that we are not able to achieve that full understanding while on earth, but we can know without a doubt that God "makes all things beautiful in His time" (Ecclesiastes 3:11). *Oh, Lord, bless us abundantly with the sweet fruit of perseverance!*

Size Isn't Everything

Triumphant faith not only enables us to persevere but also to live life well, to enter into each day with energy and an eagerness to see what God will do. Triumphant faith isn't reserved for saints or missionaries or other supergodly people; it's for all of us who want to experience to the fullest everything God has in store.

In the gospel of Matthew Jesus said, "I tell you the truth, if you have faith as small as a mustard seed, you can say to this mountain, 'Move from here to there' and it will move. Nothing will be impossible for you" (17:20). Oh boy, that sounds so simple, and yet we know that dreams don't always come true, endings are not always happy, and prayers for the sick don't always lead to physical healing. But none of those realities lessen or compromise the biblical truth that God is absolutely faithful and that His gift of faith to each of us carries us through difficult, seemingly impossible seasons.

As the well-known story of David and Goliath illustrates, victory comes not to the musclebound warrior but to the faithbound soul who places his or her faith in God's unmatchable strength. It's not the size of your faith that matters, but the size of your God.

God created faith, He provides faith generously to those who ask, and He has the final word in all matters. Our lives are not governed by the nightly news, the government, the doctor, or the bank. We don't need to live as victims of haphazard circumstances, weather patterns, or political regimes. God has the last word in our lives.

I (Kathy) remember vividly a time when my prayer life consisted solely of the phrase, *Help me, God.* Depression zapped my energy and a huge fog rolled in, blocking my view of the hope that God wanted me to hold on to. I thank God for my friends who lifted my gaze back toward heaven, where our help and hope come from.

Marriage, finances, work, children, singleness, relationships, addictions, disease, emotions—all of these can create hurdles in our race of faith. But we can fly over those hurdles in triumph if we've been training properly. We need not flinch in the face of life's trials, because good athletes and warriors come prepared. In the life of faith, that preparation involves Bible study, fellowship with others, and a consistent, intimate prayer life. Got game?

Remember what we read earlier about Paul's encouragement to keep our eyes "on the goal, where God is beckoning us onward—to Jesus"? That's what triumphant faith is all about: constantly striving toward Christlikeness, toward the victory God has promised to those who give themselves fully to the work of the Lord (see 1 Corinthians 15:57–58).

So let's keep focused on that goal, those of us who want everything God has for us. If any of you have something else in mind, something less than total commitment, God will clear your blurred vision—you'll see it yet! Now that we're on the right track, let's stay on it. (Philippians 3:15–16, MSG)

Will you let God go before you, as He went before Jehoshaphat, Joseph, David, and others? "If God is for us, who can be against us?" (Romans 8:31). He never loses. He is never late. He does not look away. He has the final say in all things, and He wants to bless you with triumphant faith.

Keep your eyes on the prize, and live like a winner!

Thoughts to *Noodle* On

1. In what area(s) of life do you find it difficult to maintain a triumphant faith?

2. When you compare your faith life with Jehoshaphat's, what similarities do you notice? What differences?

3. On a scale of 1 to 10, with 10 being Joseph and 1 being Ahab, where would you rate the strength of your faith today? Explain your answer.

4. Since triumphant faith comes through preparation, in which of the following areas do you need to do some strength training: Bible study, fellowship with others, a consistent and intimate prayer life? What plan will you put in place today to get started?

Chapter 3

Faith That Translates

What you believe in your heart comes out in your life

One of the many things I (Kathy) miss about New York is the rich variety of ethnic food. There's a pizzeria on every corner and a *real* bagel store not too far from that. I also miss the directness that characterizes New Yorkers. They communicate with a certain "edge" that folks from the south tend to interpret as hardness. Really, it's more about just calling things the way we see them. If we don't like you, we won't fake it. If you ask us something, we'll tell you what we think. When you look at us funny, it bothers us—and we'll let you know.

One of my friends told me about the time she stopped in a New York bakery to get directions to a diner. The Italian owner came around the counter with an apron stretched across his big belly and a gold chain draped over his sleeveless T-shirt. He held out the palm of his hand and proceeded to draw on it with the index finger of his other hand.

"You go lika deesa." *He points.*

"Den go ova heera." *Points again.*

"Lika deesa." *Draws an imaginary line.*

"Maka lefta." *Draws some more.*

"Go ova heera." *Points.*

"It'sa ova dare!" *Index finger on "the diner" in his palm.*

My friend watched with great amusement, then told the man that she wasn't quite following. Looking annoyed, he grabbed a napkin, slapped it down in the center of his palm, and started all over again—in a louder voice.

"You go lika deesa…"

Just as any full-blooded Italian exudes a strong cultural identity that colors his or her approach to life, so our faith transforms our sense of identity and affects how we deal with our circumstances. In addition, when we feast on abundant faith, it will so permeate our beings that it richly seasons our actions and words—like freshly chopped garlic, sautéed in olive oil.

Faith translates the language of our hearts into the language of our lives. What do we mean by that? Well, let's go back to the brilliant Mr. Webster and his definitions:

> **translate,** *v.* to change from one place, condition, person to another; to put into different words

You may have guessed that the word *translate* is a cousin to the word *transfer*. They share the prefix *trans-*, which means "over, across, beyond." They are related to the notion of movement, connection, and destination, which we encounter in words like *transport, transplant, transmit*. If it's all right with you, let's discuss *trans-fats* some other time. For now, let's focus on this idea of faith that translates, changing form from something we believe into something we say and do. In other words, faith puts feet and hands and words to what we believe in ways that clearly, confidently, and respectfully communicate God's grace to everyone we encounter.

> *Il dire è una cosa, il fare è un'altra.*
> **Saying is one thing, doing another.**

This doesn't mean you have to hand out tracts to your grocery clerk or close every conversation with "God bless you," although those things may have their place. Faith that translates means living in such a way that everything you say and do in some way points to the reality that the living God is at work in you and through you. We quite like this quotation attributed to our beloved fellow countryman Saint Francis of Assisi: "Preach the gospel at all times, and when necessary use words."

Check Your Vital Signs

I (Ellie) have spent this past autumn teaching the book of James to the (mostly) blond women of the Bright Pond Bible Study, a neighborhood gathering of four women that began in my home ten years ago and has since grown. Normally, this is the highlight of my week, but I must confess I find James to be rather unpleasant company at times.

The book of James is called the "Proverbs of the New Testament," and with good reason. Jesus's half-brother James offers five brief chapters chock full of clear, pull-no-punch directives for how we are to live.

Quite candidly, I'm not thrilled with everything James has to say. I mean, really. Who wants to hear that we're to "consider it pure joy" (1:2) when we face trials of many kinds? A dot of joy or obedient joy, I could go with—but *pure* joy? Later James throws in a reminder of the fleeting nature of life on this planet: "You are just a vapor" (4:14, NASB). That's not an easy perspective to maintain when I'm stressed out by house leaks, holiday décor, college searches, or endless to-do lists.

Every week, I find myself repenting of what I am doing wrong according to the particular portion of Scripture we're studying. We just covered the taming of the tongue. Oh brother. Somebody get me a big stapler and we'll be done with it! (No, not to staple the Bible closed—just my mouth.) James says that those who claim to be religious but do not control their tongues deceive themselves (see 1:26). I love God, I really do. But my tongue has gone its own way on more occasions than I care to count. Still, who am I to pick and choose which Bible verses sit well with me?

Anyway, James's writing centers on the theme that "faith, if it has no works, is dead" (2:17, NASB), and he goes on to instruct us in how to be patient in testing, how to have power over the tongue (help me, Lord!), how to be peacemakers, and how to be prayerful in times of trouble. In other words, James, along with the rest of the Bible, makes clear that faith isn't just about believing with our hearts; genuine, abundant faith translates into practical responses for just about every situation we'll ever face.

Faith Translates into Patience

> Be patient, then, brothers, until the Lord's coming. See how the farmer
> waits for the land to yield its valuable crop and how patient he is for the
> autumn and spring rains. You too, be patient and stand firm, because
> the Lord's coming is near. (James 5:7–8)

I (Ellie) rather like teaching about seeds and soil, sowing and reaping, vines and branches, roots, shoots, and fruits. But I am capable only of expounding on these things metaphorically rather than literally. Let's just say that this city-raised woman has never grown anything (unless you count three kids), and my house contains artificial plants only. The basics of agriculture elude me. I listen in awe to farm stories, mountain stories, and ranch stories from friends who grew up quite far south or west of Brooklyn, so the idea of patience as a valuable crop fascinates me even as it challenges me.

At a young age I was taught that "patience is a virtue," but I had no idea how to attain it. As a college freshman, I heard my philosophy professor quote Saint Augustine's assertion that "Patience is companion of wisdom."[1] I realized this treasured virtue was even more elusive than I'd thought, and I needed more patience to wait for wisdom to arrive. When I turned forty, a friend sent me a book of quotations, in which I found Hal Borland's take on the subject. "If you would know strength and majesty and patience, welcome the company of trees."[2] That one hit the bull's-eye of my limited brain, and I felt that I finally had a handle on the meaning of patience: the farmer is not caught up in the miniscule, painfully slow signs of growth; he waits for the harvest and keeps busy doing the right things, in and out of season.

For the Christian, patience is a fruit of the Spirit (see Galatians 5:22). It's a gift, but not one that comes easily, cheaply, or without responsibility on the part of the recipient. Putting it to work in our relationships is a particular challenge for most of us. Proverbs 19:11 states, "A man's wisdom gives him patience; it is to his glory to overlook an offense."

It's painful but truthful to share that the person who offended me most often in years past was my own father. As "daddy's little girl," I saw him through rose-colored glasses until my teenage years. Though Dad did nothing illegal or immoral, I could rehearse a long list of his offenses. In short, he was a prideful, critical, wounded, macho Italian American who was also handsome, generous, dutiful, and gifted in so many ways. Like all of us, he demonstrated a frustrating mixture of good qualities and hurtful behaviors. I do not wish to disrespect his memory, but I am so thankful for the amazing work God did in my heart so that I could love him purely and without malice.

By God's grace and my deliberate choice, I was patient with my father—as was my wonderful husband, who often reminded me of God's ways being higher than ours. I worked hard not to take offense when he spoke words that were unkind. I asked God to help me to return good when it was not given. I often prayed for help to grant forgiveness, although it was not ever asked for.

Patience is all about waiting without seeing instant results. I waited over thirty years for my dad to allow me to speak of Jesus and heaven and eternal life without his leaving the room. The softening in his final days and the letter he wrote to me from his deathbed affirmed that our love was mutual. As I tearily delivered his eulogy, I could not help but marvel that wisdom and patience had surely arrived, quietly and unannounced, while I was tending fields and spending time with trees.

Faith Translates into Care for Others

Where you have envy and selfish ambition, there you find disorder and
every evil practice. But the wisdom that comes from heaven is first of all
pure; then peace-loving, considerate, submissive, full of mercy and good
fruit, impartial and sincere. (James 3:16–17)

This passage and others like it point to the ways in which our faith should shine through our treatment of others. I don't know about you, but this area of caring relationships is one in which I often struggle.

But, Ellie, you teach a weekly Bible study, and you travel twenty weekends a year telling women across America about God's love, and you've written six books in six years. Isn't that caring for others?

Well, yes and no. The shortcomings of my personal life are directly linked to the outpouring of my public life. Frank and I strongly believe that I am called by God to be a Christian communicator, and we have agreed that God comes first, marriage second, the kids third, and then those ten other important categories follow right after.

Even so, competing priorities often leave me wondering how to juggle it all

Maria and Gina's Pizza Dough

When you need to work out your frustrations with life, trying slapping down some pizza dough.

Ingredients

- 1 packet dry active yeast
- 1 cup warm water (105 to 115 degrees)
- 1/2 teaspoon salt
- 2 teaspoons olive oil
- 1 teaspoon sugar
- 2 1/2 to 3 cups all-purpose flour
- cornmeal to sprinkle (optional)

Cooking Instructions

1. Dissolve yeast in warm water. Add salt, oil, sugar, and 2 1/2 cups flour. Mix with hands or dough hook of electric mixer until well

while nurturing my most important relationships. I don't beat myself up regularly, but I have endured a few self-pity sessions through the past eight years since my extensive travel started. I have missed recitals, games, homecomings, proms, and cast parties. I've missed weddings, birthday parties, dinner parties, and barbecues. I have also missed seeing new movies with Frank, going to the mall with my daughters, watching my son umpire little football players, and having lunch with friends. Did I mention I often miss church?

Although the demands on your time may look different from mine, I'm certain you can relate to the challenge of juggling, spinning, and maneuvering through a typical week without any of those you love feeling neglected.

During the writing of this book, Frank shared at dinner one night that he would appreciate more support for his ministry and for the kids. After initially

---

combined. Continue mixing, adding remaining flour 1 tablespoon at a time until dough forms a ball and sides of bowl are clean. Knead until elastic, about 10 minutes by hand or 2 minutes with a mixer.

2. Place dough in bowl greased with olive oil; turn to oil all sides. Cover with plastic wrap and towel, then set in a warm, draft-free area until doubled, about 1 hour.

3. Slap down dough. Lightly oil a 14-inch pizza pan or cookie sheet with olive oil or spray. Sprinkle with cornmeal. Work dough into desired shape; press dough into pan, shaping as you press into desired thickness. Form a slight collar around edges of dough to hold sauce.

4. Top as desired. Bake on bottom rack in a preheated 450-degree oven for 15 to 20 minutes. Remove, place on cutting surface, and cool slightly before serving.

Serves 4 (or 2 if you're very hungry).

becoming defensive, I prayed and realized he was being reasonable. (He always is, and that bugs me!) I decided to cut back on my speaking engagements, decline invitations to travel at Christmas, and take a sabbatical from writing. (Note to our editor: don't worry; that's after this book is finished!) I continue to be true to my promise to always be off the road from mid-May to mid-September in order to focus more fully on our family. We also reinstituted date night once a week.

Faith that translates into caring for people means "First things first," as the saying goes. Does God know that you deeply care? Do you seek Him? Do you read His Word? Do you listen for His voice? If you are married, does your mate know that you deeply care? Are you committed to the vows you took for better or worse? If you are a parent, does that child know that you deeply care? Does he or she feel your tangible support and unconditional love? Relatives, friends, neighbors, colleagues—do they know you care?

Who do we care about, and how can we show that care?

We care by praying for those who matter. We care with words, hugs, acts of service, cards, flowers, meals, gifts, phone calls, e-mails, errands, and most important, offering what Jill Briscoe calls the "ministry of presence." This very special saint speaks of the many opportunities we have to model Christ's love and care for others by going to them and simply saying, "I just had to come." It's the ministry of showing up, being there, and maybe just being quiet as you hold a hand, scrub a sink, or sit in the same room.

It is not our responsibility to take care of everyone—that's God's job—but we certainly must be open to His direction when it comes to investing our time and energy in ways that say how much we care to the people who matter most.

Faith Translates into Humility

> Everyone should be quick to listen, slow to speak and slow to become
> angry, for man's anger does not bring about the righteous life that God
> desires.... Humble yourselves before the Lord, and he will lift you up.
> (James 1:19–20; 4:10)

I (Kathy) have met a number of eloquent Christians who communicate the gospel with words both beautiful and convincing. Sadly, in many cases their lives lack the conviction and sincerity their words hold. Now don't get me wrong. I am fully aware of the hypocrisy we all battle in living out the gospel purely. But to the world, to our families, to friends who don't know the true essence of who Jesus is, those hypocrisies in all of us have stained His reputation. Faith gets lost in translation for people who have met only "do as I say but not as I do" Christians.

Jesus spoke of such hypocrites in Matthew 15:8: "These people honor me with their lips, but their hearts are far from me." By contrast, when people meet the true character of Jesus in us, He becomes irresistible and undeniable. It is one thing to share your faith and quite another thing to show your faith.

> We sincere Christians do not wish to put a stumbling block in anyone's
> path, so that our lives, our ministry, and our witness will not be discredited.
> Rather, as servants of God, we commend ourselves in every way: in great
> endurance; in troubles, in hardships, in distresses, in beatings, in imprison-
> ments, in riots; in hard work, in sleepless nights, in hunger, and also in
> purity and understanding, in patience and kindness; in the Holy Spirit and
> in sincere love; in truthful speech and in the power of God. We do *all* of
> this with weapons of righteousness in the right hand and in the left; through
> glory and dishonor, through bad reports and good reports; we are genuine,
> yet regarded as imposters; known, yet regarded as strangers; dying, and
> yet we live on; beaten, and yet not killed; sorrowful, yet always rejoicing;
> poor, yet making many rich; having nothing, and yet possessing everything.
> (2 Corinthians 6:3–10, paraphrased)

Faith in Jesus gives us the motivation to operate in ways that stand out in a world obsessed with looking out for number one. When you view this life from an eternal perspective, everything is filtered through that lens. You see that another One is in control. Another One will have the last say. Another One has your very best interest at heart.

Last year a group of special women gathered together for Ellie's fiftieth birthday. We spent a weekend together eating, laughing, sharing, and touring the Library of Congress and the National Gallery of Art. A couple of weeks before our get-together, a few women e-mailed me to see if the no-gift policy was firm. I assured them that the pleasure of their company was the best gift of all. I did, however, remind them of Ellie's deep love for words and how much it would delight her if each of us would express our appreciation and love for her in that way. We shared our sentiments after dinner one night, and it was such a precious time. Ellie was deeply moved, and I wondered why most of us do not do this more often. Why do we wait for a crisis or a eulogy?

Then much to our surprise, Ellie asked all of us to take off our shoes. As we obliged, she left the room and reentered with a basin, a pitcher of water, and some washcloths. We were there to celebrate her life, but she had planned to celebrate ours. She went around the room, knelt before each woman, and as she washed each friend's feet, she affirmed her life, her character, and her purpose by humbly, tangibly showing us God's love. It was a deeply moving experience.

What Ellie did for me personally that day was remind me to continue to humble myself and serve in any way that glorifies God.

That is what faith does. It takes our focus off ourselves and puts it on others. I couldn't help but think of Jesus, the King of kings, bowing down to wash the feet of His friends. He showed us that we are to take every opportunity to sacrificially love and count others more worthy than ourselves.

Faith Translates into an Active Prayer Life

> Is any one of you in trouble? He should pray.... Is any one of you sick? He should call the elders of the church to pray over him and anoint him with oil in the name of the Lord.... Therefore confess your sins to each other and pray for each other so that you may be healed. The prayer of a righteous man is powerful and effective. (James 5:13–14, 16)

I (Kathy) remember how I used to pray as a child and young woman before I actually knew *who* I was praying to. I hoped that someone would hear. I thought I *should* pray in case there was even a slight chance that God was really listening. Maybe something I said or asked for would make its way to heaven's doors. Maybe Saint Peter would find it on one of his sticky notes beneath the pile of prayers he'd deliver to God's secretary. Still I wondered if God would ever get my request. Surely it would be lost or forgotten amid the endless demands He received in the course of one day.

Let's *Dish* About...
Taming Your Tongue

EL: As an outspoken Italian, when do you find it most difficult to tame your tongue?

KT: I have the hardest time when I am provoked. When someone else's words are prodding at me—*jab, jab, jab*—my initial reaction is to come back with a quick and powerful right hook.

EL: So how do you speak from faith instead of anger or frustration?

KT: It comes down to regaining my spiritual sanity. I mentally remove myself from the moment and take a breath until I can respond with wisdom and love. Because I have suffered a great deal in the past from having to clean up the carnage I've created in a war of words, I'm trying to be more conscious about being a woman of few words in tense conversations. I've seen how words kill and destroy.

EL: I know what you mean. I have to keep reminding myself of Matthew 5:7, where Jesus said, "Blessed are the merciful, for they will be shown mercy." When I think about the mercy I need from God, that helps seal my lips in a hurry!

As I look back, it saddens me that I did not have a clue as to how real and kind and loving God is. Now I know and rejoice that throughout the Scriptures the Lord invites us to come to Him, to worship Him, to rest with Him, to cry out to Him, and even to reason with Him. I love that!

He continually invites us to intimacy. That is why religion in and of itself can be so dangerous. It often takes relationship with God out of the equation of our faith. When you truly know someone and love someone, the thought of being away from or not speaking to that person is painful. It is the same with Jesus. That's why faith in Him translates into an active prayer life.

When you know that God is as real and constant as the air we breathe, that He hears and is consistently there—"Where can I flee from your presence?" (Psalm 139:7)—faith can't help but speak to Him not only in the hard times but through-out the course of the day.

Recently as I was working in my office, three different scenarios arose within just a couple of hours that caused me stress and anguish. Each time I laid my head down and offered Him my prayer. Lately, I have been more and more conscious of giving over to the Lord every concern rather than letting them pierce my heart, where they will only cause fear and despair.

We should make a habit of coming to God about everything, allowing faith to translate our pain and anxiety into prayer. And in doing so, we will find great peace and comfort and hope.

All the Help We Can Get

We could spend the rest of our lives becoming aligned with the helpful (and mandatory) instructions the Lord gives through His faithful servant James. But we can only accomplish this with humility, grace, and the help of the Holy Spirit.

Hebrews 11:6 tells us, "Without faith it is impossible to please God." That is a big "ouch!" for me (Ellie) because I would like to be able to please God on my own merit and win favor with people at the same time. When I do or say the right thing, my first reaction sometimes is to look up and say, "Hey, God, did You notice how humble I was just then?" or, "Lord, did You hear my holy response when that neighbor shared that snide remark? Pretty good, huh?" I want Him to pat my back when I give to the poor or underprivileged, to give me an "Attagirl" when I resist the temptation to say something sharp to one of the kids. In reality, "there is only One who is good" (Matthew 19:17). Faith leaves no room for personal pride because it knows, as Paul observed, "It is God who works in you to will and to act according to his good purpose" (Philippians 2:13).

Keeping God at the center of our lives isn't easy amid the distractions of iPods and BlackBerries, chocolate and coffee, CNN and the Food Network, office meetings and family squabbles, or whatever else tends to grab our attention. But this challenge isn't unique to our modern existence; from the beginning of time people have struggled with the temptation to think the world exists not for God's purposes but for their own self-focused fulfillment. Think Adam and Eve, Cain and Abel, the Tower of Babel.

For this reason the Jewish teachers had much to say about how to achieve a faith-centered life. Proverbs 3:3 says, "Let love and faithfulness never leave you; bind them around your neck, write them on the tablet of your heart." Some observant Jews wear tefellin, small leather pouches containing scrolls of Torah passages, tied around their arms and foreheads. These are meant to serve as constant reminders of God's presence and His mitzvot, the 613 commandments Jews are obligated to observe, according to Jewish tradition.

As modern women, we tend to click on all the Internet articles that tell us how to unclutter our lives rather than looking for more things to carry around with us. But would having the Ten Commandments—or even just the two greatest ones—tied around our foreheads help us think more often about living in ways that please God?

Here's good news for those of us who have enough trouble keeping track of our overloaded handbags without having to worry about a small leather pouch: as followers of God, we constantly carry around with us absolutely everything we need for the life of faith in the form of the Holy Spirit, whom we can never misplace.

In our current culture, being a spiritual person is considered chic, a basic requirement for anyone who aspires to be deeper than a paper cut. Many mistakenly think of this person of the Trinity as a ghost or an angel or a warm fuzzy feeling. Or they think that any of the spirits hanging around can serve as a guide.

In truth there is only one Holy Spirit, God Himself—God in us. Scripture teaches that the same Spirit who raised Christ from the dead is the Spirit who desires to reside in each one of us (see Romans 8:11). Want personal power? Ignore those hyped infomercials and become acquainted with the Holy Spirit of God instead. He is your Advocate, always reminding the Father of your place in the family. While Satan, the false Accuser, whispers lies to you and about you, the Holy Spirit rebuffs him and reminds him that you belong to God. He has never lost a case. The Holy Spirit is the great Comforter, whose presence can settle your soul like nothing and no one else ever can.

> If you then, though you are evil, know how to give good gifts to your children, how much more will your Father in heaven give the Holy Spirit to those who ask him! (Luke 11:13)

The constant presence of the Holy Spirit is God's gracious gift to guide us into truth (see John 16:13), to encourage us (see Acts 9:31), to fill our hearts with His love (see Romans 5:5). And that's just for starters. The Spirit also nurtures within us those characteristics that are essential to living out our faith in tangible ways: love, joy, peace, patience, kindness, goodness, faithfulness, gentleness, and self-control (see Galatians 5:22–23).

We can't speak for you, but in those areas we need all the help we can get.

Gotta Tell Somebody

Another major role the Holy Spirit plays is in giving us the courage to boldly tell others where we get the strength to respond gently to a rude clerk, to stay calm when the oven conks out the day before Thanksgiving, to exude an air of grace—or at least a semblance of sanity—when we're stuck on the tarmac for hours on end.

We can already hear you quibbling with us: "But I'm not like you two colorful Italians; I'm just a quiet, private person. I don't have the gift of evangelism." Hey, we understand. Our quiet moments may be few, but we know what it's like to be so talked out that we sometimes hope that we don't have to make conversation with the people next to us. But that doesn't negate the challenge that when you have feasted on faith, you should want to share a generous serving with the hungry souls around you.

Those who physically witnessed Jesus performing miracles were compelled to tell others what they saw. That's human nature. The more astounding an incident is, the more intent we are in passing it on. The same is true for a product, service, restaurant, medical treatment, or vacation spot we have loved or benefited from. We want to tell somebody about it. We pass along certain information we believe would help others. My (Ellie's) aunts in Brooklyn used to call each other whenever there was a good sale on tomatoes. We don't want to keep a good tip to ourselves! And that is the very reason for what the church calls evangelism.

Sure, it sounds religious, but it's just a formal word for telling people about who God is and what He did through the Red Sea, across the Jordan River, in a manger in Bethlehem, on a terrible Good Friday, and in your heart. The word *evangelism* is not found in the Bible, but it was clearly mandated by Jesus:

You will receive power when the Holy Spirit comes on you; and you
will be my witnesses in Jerusalem, and in all Judea and Samaria, and
to the ends of the earth. (Acts 1:8)

Therefore go and make disciples of all nations, baptizing them
in the name of the Father and of the Son and of the Holy Spirit.
(Matthew 28:19)

A disciple is a student, a learner, a follower. How can people follow Jesus if they do not hear about Him, if they do not learn about Him from us? "How, then, can they call on the one they have not believed in? And how can they believe in the one of whom they have not heard? And how can they hear without someone preaching to them?" (Romans 10:14). Faith doesn't come magically or through osmosis; it comes as the Holy Spirit gives us words to say and then touches the hearts of those listening to respond to the truth we have spoken: "The Holy Spirit will teach you at that time what you should say" (Luke 12:12).

Translating your faith into words isn't about your ability (the Holy Spirit takes care of that) but about your willingness. And being willing to tell others about

Jesus doesn't automatically mean you'll be called to overseas missions service either. God calls only a few to journey to far-flung places; more often His Spirit compels us to…

- walk across the street to the home where a domestic disturbance brought a visit from the police the previous night
- visit the young Christian girl who feels trapped in an out-of-wedlock pregnancy
- step into the next cubicle, where an overwhelmed co-worker is dealing with the devastation of bad news

How prepared are we to share the radical, life-altering story of Jesus Christ? Are we willing to be more astute students of His Word in order to intelligently, logically walk a person through the plan of salvation? Are we willing to be transparent in sharing our own personal story of transformation and healing?

Here's our favorite definition of evangelism: one beggar showing another where the free banquet is. We may be intimidated by the Four Spiritual Laws or stumble over the Romans Road, but we can and must translate our faith into words as we tell others what Jesus has done in our own lives.

What's Your Story?

The esteemed Christian psychologist Dr. Dan Allender penned a book titled *To Be Told: Know Your Story, Shape Your Future.* In it, he implores us not to miss our own story as we get caught up reading and watching everybody else's story. He explains that God is not only our authority but also our author. Each of us, including you, has a story—and our stories need to be told. You may not be a historian, a sociologist, or a Bible scholar, but you have a story to tell, and no one can tell it but you!

Friends, co-workers, and family members may hotly debate your "religious" habits, your attendance at Bible study, and your literal interpretation of the Ten Commandments, but no one can argue with *your* story. Your changed habits, your renewed sense of hope, and your emotional healing speak clearly of a God who has not put His quill down. The unmerited kindness, forgiveness, and mercy you show to both intimates and strangers in your life speak boldly of the God you have come to see with new eyes. What powerful billboards we can be for a risen Savior! But how will they know if we don't care enough to share?

If Not You, Who?

We realize that in these days when tolerance is one of our society's highest values, it has become fashionable to be intolerant of those who want to talk about their faith. But God's love working in and through us compels us to share our faith with those whose souls are hungry for truth.

For example, I (Ellie) once searched out a funky art studio near the harbor of historic Alexandria, just south of DC. I was there to have a broken but valuable glass sculpture repaired by a master artisan. As he administered fire, water, sand, and chemicals to my prized piece of glass, he told me his story. He'd been a struggling artist for many years until he created a shrine to the "Glass Goddess" in his backyard. He leaned a bottle of gin against the handcrafted idol and "soon learned that she was a party animal." He told me he replaces the gin bottle every month, and the studio has increased in business ever since. *And I shouldn't share my story?*

Another day the Turkish woman giving me a manicure began to weep as she relayed the details of the skin disease, slow death, and burial of her beloved mother near the Black Sea. Though she missed her mom, she cried more over the thought of her mother being eaten by worms and awaiting another life in the cold dirt. She hoped that her mother would soon be "assigned" another life form. *And I shouldn't share my story?*

On a two-hour flight I found myself next to a young man covered in piercings and tattoos. When I sincerely inquired as to the meaning of some, the nineteen-year-old gladly described for me his convoluted, narcissistic, hedonistic, white-supremacist worldview. *And I shouldn't share my story?*

A friend introduced me to a beautiful and intelligent woman who enjoys all the trimmings and accoutrements of suburban life. Or does she? After several social encounters, it became painfully evident that she was gripped with fear, feeling trapped in a loveless marriage and resorting to harmful habits to numb the pain from living a masquerade. She sincerely hoped her husband would have an affair so that she could leave and feel exonerated. She stays because of the kids. *And I shouldn't share my story?*

Our Fairfax County public school system is sending home flyers and booklets about helping children cope with the aftermath of terrorism, natural disasters, gang activity, and school shootings. They specifically suggest "The Turtle Method" for children dealing with fear and anxiety. In this counselor-sanctioned exercise, the kids can pretend they are turtles, go into their shells, and breathe deeply while imagining they are somewhere else. This is the best expertise they have to share with our children. *And I shouldn't share my story?*

Going Out on Faith

An integral part of my story is being a native New Yorker and now a resident of the metro Washington DC area these past fourteen years. On that sunny, perfect, blue sky morning of September 11, 2001, the phone rang just as I got the three children off to school. It was Kathy, crying and telling me to turn on the television. We wept together for the next hour and a half.

I wanted it to be a Spielberg movie that could be rewound and edited. I wanted the "special effects" to be deleted. I wanted it to not be true. I wanted a huge safety net to catch all the people who jumped from the towers to escape the engulfing flames. I wanted to know what it all meant for my world and my country and my family. What I got was a sharp ache in my heart and a sick feeling in the pit of my stomach.

Soon every other channel was telecasting footage of my beautiful hometown, which now looked war torn and apocalyptic. And my newly adopted city of Washington looked kicked and beaten down at our very fortress of power and might. A charred crater in a Pennsylvania field bore witness to more loss and despair.

You may recall that Todd Beamer was one of the heroes on Flight 93 and that his words, "Let's roll," became the rallying cry for the nation. However, the most poignant words Todd uttered that fateful day are buried in the transcript of the recording between Todd and Lisa Jefferson, a supervisor with GTE Airfone. Just before reciting the Lord's Prayer together and in what must have been an excruciating moment, Todd said to Lisa, "I don't think we're going to get out of this thing. I'm going to have to go out on faith."[3] I have been deeply impacted by those words. How insightful, profound, philosophical, and truly accurate Todd Beamer was in his final observation.

Did he realize he was speaking for all of humanity? None of us are going to "get out of" a face-to-face confrontation with death. We're going to have to go out on faith. The birth-to-death ratio is fairly impressive; I believe it's one for one. No one lives forever. Even Lazarus had to die again! And that is why God sent His only Son to live among us, to take our sins upon Himself, to die on a cross, to be raised from the dead, and to rule and reign forever and ever.

Placing ourselves in the will of God is the *only* way we can "go out on faith." But how can others do the same unless they encounter faith alive and active in us? Will we allow them to continue on toward certain disaster without our at least *trying* to extend the truth they need?

Recently, I was drawn to a full-page photo in a world-missions magazine that depicted an Arab man walking alone over the rippled desert sands. Printed across the top of the page was a quotation identified as an ancient Arab proverb: "The greatest crime in the desert is to find water and keep silent." It was truly an "I hear you, Lord" moment for me.

When you find a source of water in a parched land, it would be cruel, criminal, and unconscionable not to tell others. And in a world gasping for hope, why would we hold back the refreshing, revitalizing truth of God's love?

In the fourth chapter of the gospel of John, a poignant exchange between Jesus and a woman at a well reinforces His identity as the only One who satisfies completely, the One who quenches the human thirst for hope. He was sitting by a well, waiting for the return of the disciples, when a Samaritan woman—a woman whose life had been one long search for lasting love—came to draw water. When Jesus said to her, "Will you give me a drink?" she pointed out that maybe she wasn't the kind of person He'd want to be served by. But Jesus was about to change her story forever.

> Jesus answered, "Everyone who drinks this water will be thirsty again, but whoever drinks the water I give him will never thirst. Indeed, the water I give him will become in him a spring of water welling up to eternal life."
>
> The woman said to him, "Sir, give me this water so that I won't get thirsty and have to keep coming here to draw water."

As their conversation continued, the Samaritan woman realized she was standing face to face with the God of her dreams. Did she keep this incredible encounter a secret, hoarding the living water for herself? No, this woman who most likely had been despised by all her neighbors for her messed-up choices ran back into town, told everyone what had happened, and brought them to meet Jesus for themselves. "Many of the Samaritans from that town believed in him because of the woman's testimony." (See John 4:6–39.)

How many will believe because of the testimony of your life, the truth in your words, the love in your heart?

The Clock
Is Running

Life seems to be moving at breakneck speed, and too many people have resigned and reduced themselves to a regimen where they punch a clock, fill in the obvious blanks, live for the weekends, and find eventual rest near a lake or a golf course. Is that all there is? Lord, forbid it! Those who possess triumphant, victorious, overcoming, life-giving faith have a mission far greater than personal comfort, regular naps, and bonbon consumption. Our hurting world needs the good news of God's grace and mercy, but we don't have a lot of time in which to spread the word. Amy Carmichael said, "We shall have all eternity to celebrate the victories, but we have only the few hours before sunset in which to win them."[4]

Can you imagine having the cure for cancer and not sharing it? In the same way, the Christian understands that there is a cure for the sickness of sin, a cure that not only brings great joy on earth but also offers a lifeline to a joyful eternity free of sorrow, sickness, or suffering. Those of us who have tasted the healing waters of God's mercy must lead others to the river of life so that they, too, may heal, live, and prosper. Our faith must translate into both actions and words that unmistakably declare our belief in a God who satisfies and fills like nothing else ever can.

Let's live in such a way that others will be irresistibly drawn to join us at the table God has prepared and to drink in the abundant, life-giving water that only He can provide.

Thoughts to *Noodle* On

1. Do you tend to preach the gospel more through your actions or through your words? Explain your answer.

2. Describe a time when the Holy Spirit's presence within you was the only possible explanation for your behavior.

3. Which chapter(s) of your own faith story have you hesitated to share with others? Why?

4. Name at least one person within your circle of influence—in your neighborhood, in your family, on the PTA, at the office—with whom you will talk this week about the difference Jesus makes in your life.

Secondi Piatti ■ Second Course

Abundant Hope

Hope is faith holding out its hand in the dark.

—GEORGE ILES

Chapter 4

Hope Has a Name

*It really is all about who you know—
and how well you know Him*

I n my (Kathy's) bedroom, in a beautiful museum-mounted frame, hangs a pair of black gloves given to Judy Garland during the making of *A Star Is Born*—a gift from Ellie for my fortieth birthday. She knows I've always been fascinated by the passionate and dynamic and vulnerable Judy, who sang her heart out with every fiber of her being.

Unknowingly, Judy Garland presented me with a life-giving gift when I was six years old. She sang to me from a farm in Kansas and told me that somewhere over the rainbow skies were blue…and that the dreams I'd dare to dream really would come true. I thought my heart would burst within me the very first time I watched *The Wizard of Oz*. Even though I was surrounded by my extended—and extensive—Italian family, I felt lonely. I wondered what awaited beyond the boundaries of my limited world. Even though I was a mere child, my deepest soul longed for something higher and wider and everlasting. Judy touched that hope with her voice and assured me that one day I would find that *something*.

My girlish yearnings reflected the need for hope that lies within all of us. Hope propels us to act, to dream, to write, to love, to live life to the fullest. Hope is what inspires us to get out of bed each morning, to take another breath in the midst of deep pain, not knowing what each day will hold. It puts the wind in the sails of our souls. This kind of hope isn't simply...

- *I hope it doesn't rain.*
- *I hope we get there in time.*
- *I hope he asks me out.*
- *I hope he leaves me alone!*

The hope that leads to abundant life is confident. A hope assured. Underneath the many different notes of hope that shape the melodies of our lives plays one major theme: *I hope my life means something, that I matter.* And a voice quietly sings in response, *You matter so much, I love you so much...that I died for you. I am the Hope you're looking for.*

Putting a Name to Our Hope

In 1 Peter 1:3 we read, "Praise be to the God and Father of our Lord Jesus Christ! In his great mercy he has given us new birth into a living hope through the resurrection of Jesus Christ from the dead."

A living hope. What beautiful words. In Jesus Christ we have access to hope that is real, tangible, alive. Colossians 1:27 says this: "Christ in you, the hope of glory." Hope has a name: *Christ in you.*

The hope of our hearts isn't answered by a God sitting off somewhere on a big mountain where thousands line up to make their requests. We don't find our hope in some cosmic Yoda-like teacher of wisdom. Our hope hangs on a God who sent Jesus to show us what He looks like and then sent the Holy Spirit to guide us and keep us through this earthly life. He actually told us He would come and live inside us and comfort us. How utterly amazing that the Spirit who raised Jesus now lives in us!

This is the essence of hope: that God came to us through Jesus, that He died for our sins, that He rose from the grave having conquered sin and death, and that because of the Resurrection we can have a personal relationship with Immanuel, "God with us" (Matthew 1:23).

Something About That Name!

When the angel appeared to Joseph to reassure him about Mary's unexpected pregnancy, his message included these words: "She will give birth to a son, and you are to give him the name Jesus, because he will save his people from their sins" (Matthew 1:21). *Give him the name Jesus, because he will save.* The name of Jesus saves. It rescues. It drags us from the muck and mire of the deepest pit and places us back on solid ground and eventually on a mountaintop. The name of Jesus is an endless reserve of comfort and peace because it possesses the very essence of hope. "We have put our hope in the living God, who is the Savior of all men, and especially of those who believe" (1 Timothy 4:10).

The eighteenth-century pastor Edward Mote wrote a hymn that perfectly captures the nature of the hope we have in Jesus:

My hope is built on nothing less
Than Jesus' blood and righteousness.
I dare not trust the sweetest frame,
But wholly lean on Jesus' name.[1]

This is where we find our hope fulfilled: by calling on the name of Jesus and centering our lives on all that His name means. There is so much power in the name of Jesus. Some days when I (Kathy) am stressed, unnerved, or angry, I will whisper His name—"Jesus, Jesus"—and something supernatural transpires. When you pray, saying His name, all of heaven takes notice. Hope pours down from the throne of God and spills throughout every corner of your heart.

The hope that God Almighty gives through His Son, Jesus, is a hope like no other. This is a hope that is guaranteed, a hope that is boldly assured. Unlike a close-your-eyes-and-wish-as-hard-as-you-can sort of hope, the hope Jesus gives is already a reality. Why? Because He has already conquered sin and death and everything else that once held the power to harm us.

The Wonder-Working Power of Hope in Jesus

Consider for a moment all that Jesus endured to give us hope, as described in 1 Peter 2. Though He was perfect and sinless, He endured public humiliation and

Let's *Dish* About...
When Hope Seems Lost

EL: Can you describe a particular time when a hopeless-looking situation turned around, all because of Jesus?

KT: When I first gave my life over to the Lord, my family was convinced I had joined a cult. My uncles would come to my house and give me a speech about my father rolling over in his grave. One aunt was particularly vocal in telling me that I was going in a wrong direction. It was such a hard season for me, and the hurt of those years lingered with me even though I stayed in relationship with everyone.

When that vocal aunt lay dying of breast cancer some years ago, I went to the hospital to visit, as all the relatives were doing. I'd just stand quietly at the end of the bed, feeling a wall because of those past conversations and knowing how she felt about my faith. I was there physically but kept my heart at a distance. Then during one of the visits, her son (my cousin) said, "Why doesn't Kathleen pray?" That blew my mind! I led the family around her bed in prayer, which was just amazing.

That incident moved me to go back another day when I was able to be alone in the room with my aunt. We had the most incredibly sweet time. I talked to her about Jesus. I explained about heaven and His love, and I asked if she'd like to invite Him into her heart. Then I held her hand and she prayed with me. To me that was absolutely miraculous. I left that hospital room so hopeful and absolutely certain that God can turn anything around.

EL: You're exactly right. Last year, a woman I'll call Karen came to the Bible study I teach at the urging—maybe it was coercion?—of a close friend. For the first few weeks she sat with her arms folded tightly and her face frozen in a grim expression. When she announced to me that she was "checking this Christian thing out," I assured her she had come to a safe place to do so.

A month later, she appeared at my front door, visibly shaken, flushed, and on the verge of angry tears. She explained that a judge had just ruled for her grandchildren to spend more time with her son's ex-wife, a woman she knew to be abusive. Because of my leadership role in Bright Pond Bible Study, she assumed that I wielded some type of influence with local leaders. Although I assured her I had none, she insisted that I "must know somebody." Her pain was palpable, and I felt so helpless. After explaining once more that I did not know anyone powerful in the county or the court, I went on to tell her that we could go to the ultimate Authority of the highest court. I offered to pray. Karen was not in the mood for such talk and abruptly left, shaking her head and audibly questioning what prayer could possibly do for those three little girls. In her opinion, I had nothing to offer her that day.

I went ahead and prayed on my own. Thankfully, Karen returned to Bible study a few weeks later. In the nine months since that conversation on my doorstep, Karen has seen God's hand move in unexpected and amazing ways on behalf of her son and her precious granddaughters. She now smiles broadly and greets me warmly each week. Best of all, she has come to understand that she knows Somebody very important in a very high place. That's what hope can do!

accusations. He was beaten, spit upon, reviled. Yet He suffered it all in silence, bearing the misery for our sakes. Then, as He hung on the cross in our place, He experienced the worst pain of all: separation from the heavenly Father, who averted His holy eyes from the One who bore all our sins in Himself. He submitted to all this willingly, "so we could be rid of sin, free to live the right way" (1 Peter 2:24, MSG).

The crucifixion of Jesus was a high-profile, public execution, and witnesses had no doubt whatsoever that His life and breath had been sucked out of Him. What persecutors like Herod, Pontius Pilate, and Caesar didn't know and were too arrogant to foresee was that His death and resurrection would only serve to ignite faith and fervor for Jesus's heavenly kingdom to the far corners of their earthly kingdoms. After the Resurrection and before He ascended into heaven, Jesus physically appeared to hundreds of people, and those encounters sparked overwhelming passion in believers and radical transformation in those who converted in the months and decades that followed. That resulting zeal, rooted in unshakable hope, is what carried the first-century Christians through unspeakable persecution and suffering. Once you've seen a man raised from the dead (or heard the vivid details firsthand), it certainly changes your worldview and rearranges your priorities.

Two thousand years later, the name of Jesus still causes quite a stir, and the reality of His living presence causes hope to bloom in the most unlikely places. Through the hope-drenched name of Jesus, the impossible is made possible:

A lame man rises and walks.
A blind woman gains her sight.
A tumor disappears.
The sinner becomes a preacher.
An addict becomes a counselor.
A prisoner becomes a mentor.
Broken marriages are restored.
Hardened, wayward teens come home to be held.
Friends are reunited.
Haunted memories are healed.

The past is redeemed.
Lives are fully transformed
through miracles of forgiveness
and repentance
and revival.

Though neither of us were witnesses to Calvary or the empty tomb, we have indeed been firsthand witnesses to everything mentioned here, along with countless other examples of how Jesus salvages the past, secures the future, and saturates the present with hope.

The Long Arms of Hope

Few of us make it far in life without some measure of pain and regret. How often have you looked at old photos of yourself sporting disco duds, sky blue shaded eyes, or a feathered hairdo borrowed from one of Charlie's Angels and wondered, *What was I thinking?* Or are we the only ones who cringe at the painful visions that haunt our memories as we watch all those fashion faux pas cycling back around? I (Kathy) remember when I first moved to Nashville in the early eighties. Amid all the Gloria Vanderbilt khakis and pearls, I sported a gold fingernail on my pinkie and proudly wore an Italian princess necklace given to me by my mother.

Sadly, most of us have made mistakes even worse than wearing our permed hair cement-sprayed into a three-foot tower. We've spoken hurtful or judgmental words that damaged relationships. We've made choices that sabotaged our bodies, careers, or self-esteem. And we've allowed dreams to slip away because we were too fearful to follow through.

In addition, we bear the scars of personal suffering and loss. I endured a painful struggle with depression and bulimia that lasted more years than I care to count, and I'll tell you more about that later. For now, let me just say that I know—oh yes, I know—how easy it is to be overwhelmed by the past, by all the things that *might* have been. But I have learned that hope is the dream of a brighter tomorrow past the reality of yesterday and today. It is the expectation of a new way—a new day.

In Romans we find the secret to how God brings fresh, living hope out of the darkest, deadest places in our past: "Suffering produces perseverance; perseverance, character; and character, hope; and hope does not disappoint us" (5:3–5). In other words, God doesn't waste our pain. He stretches us in our pain, increasing our capacity to be filled with His love and mercy.

Anguish in different places in my own life has enlarged my heart. My suffering has made me more compassionate. It has made me so much more sensitive to the pain of others. I have come to deeply understand what it feels like to be in bondage and how difficult it is to gain freedom. When I see people struggling with their weight or an addiction, I have such compassion for them. When I see people in the midst of depression, my heart breaks. Because I have some understanding of their pain, I don't lightly suggest an antidote or resort to Christian cliché answers. But as gently as I can, I try to turn their eyes to the hope that is Jesus, whose reach extends far enough to heal the past and shape the future.

I have found that when I sing and when I speak, comfort and hope ooze from my scars, from the very places where I have suffered most. God's light shines out of those dark caves of my life to show others the path of hope. That is just how He works: He transforms our most devastating times into divine moments of healing and wisdom and growth. That is what God does for us, just as He used the devastation of Christ's crucifixion to replace the darkness of our sins with the glory of resurrected life.

Resurrection Power Knows No Bounds

Because of Jesus and the Resurrection, we have supernatural hope for a new day. Frederick Buechner describes hope this way:

> The worst thing isn't the last thing about the world. It's the next to last
> thing. The last thing is the best. It is the power from on high that comes
> down into the world, that wells up from the rock-bottom worst of the
> world like a hidden spring.[2]

The worst thing it not the last thing! There will always be an Easter Sunday, no matter how bad Good Friday gets. God gives us the gift of morning after the dark and terrifying night. When all seems lost, we can know a new day is coming. "The LORD says, 'Forget what happened before, and do not think about the past. Look at the new thing I am going to do. It is already happening. Don't you see it?'" (Isaiah 43:18–19, NCV).

You may scoff at the idea of forgetting the past, convinced that its shadow will always hang over you. You may be thinking…

- *You don't understand. I was abused by my parents, my boyfriend.*
- *You don't understand. I was a complete mess as a parent.*
- *You don't understand. I was an unfaithful wife.*
- *You don't understand. I was an alcoholic, a drug addict, a pill popper.*
- *You don't understand. I was rejected by my family.*
- *You don't understand. I was abandoned by my husband.*
- *You don't understand. I was raped.*

You're absolutely right; we cannot fully understand all you've been through. But God does, and we're here to tell you that He is the God of the impossible. Whenever you look at yourself in the light of the past, we urge you to say this: "I was, but God is!" He is the Redeemer, and He makes all things new. If you let Him, God will use the pain of your past to fulfill the promise of your future. He is the living Hope.

Hope has a name: Christ in you, the hope of glory. That Hope is trustworthy. But most times we need to wait as we hope and trust. Author and speaker Ken Gire wrote about this:

How do we get to the morning, to the sunshine, to the joy? There is only one way. By waiting for it. We can't hurry the dawn no matter how anxiously we pace the floor or how impatiently we watch the clock. And so the question is not, do we wait or not wait, because waiting is all we can do. The question is, how will we wait? Will we wait well…or will we wait poorly?[3]

So many turn away from God or grow bitter during the wait. A sad, sad life flows from that kind of existence. I (Kathy) have learned all too often that God will not always deliver me from my pain, but He will be there through it. I remember when I found out that my mother had six months to live. *Am I not still God?* He whispered to my spirit. After gut-wrenching cries and teeth-clenched anger, I answered yes. I could have dragged bitterness into my mother's room during her few short days left on this planet. But most days, peace, hope, and comfort flowed from my heart to hers because I knew she was in bigger hands than mine. My sister and I spoon-fed her Jesus, and although she got to the point where she couldn't eat food, she was filled to the brim with Him. When she finally closed her eyes and went from what I call "life to life," I felt the deepest sorrow but the truest peace.

We need to remember that the miracle of the Resurrection took place three days after an agonizing crucifixion. For three days Jesus's followers believed all hope was gone. Three days of grieving, regrets, and sorrow. Then at last came the glorious news: He is risen. "Death has been swallowed up in victory" (1 Corinthians 15:54).

Pia's Polenta and Vegetables

This tasty dish will help you meet your veggie require-
ments for the day.

Ingredients

- 2 tablespoons extra-virgin olive oil
- 1 medium eggplant, chopped
- 1 medium zucchini, chopped
- 1/2 teaspoon salt
- 1/2 teaspoon freshly ground pepper
- 1/2 cup water
- 10 ounces baby spinach
- 1 1/2 cups prepared marinara (meatless)
  sauce
- 1/2 cup chopped fresh basil
- 14 ounces prepared polenta (box or tube)
- 1 1/2 cups shredded mozzarella, divided
  (part skim suggested)

If you are in a waiting period right now, let us reassure you that the Resurrection will come. Resurrection never comes without the passion, without the pain. That is part of the mystery of God. Embrace the Cross, and you get the Resurrection.

Hope Rewrites Our Future

As we shared in the last chapter, everyone has a story. The chapters in our lives are being penned with the inks of both joy and sorrow. The good news is that our stories are constantly being written. God never puts His pen down. He weaves twists and turns, excitement and tragedy through the pages of our lives, creating brilliant plots and adventures. It is so hard to see the beauty of the story in the making when

Cooking Instructions

1. Preheat oven to 450 degrees. Coat a 9 x 13-inch baking dish with cooking spray.
2. Heat oil in a large nonstick skillet over medium-high heat. Add eggplant, zucchini, salt, and pepper. Cook, stirring occasionally, until vegetables are tender and just beginning to brown, 4 to 6 minutes.
3. Add water and spinach; cover and cook until spinach is wilted, about 3 minutes, stirring once. Stir marinara sauce into vegetables and heat through, 1 to 2 minutes. Remove from heat and stir in basil.
4. Place polenta slices in a single layer in prepared baking dish, trimming to fit if necessary. Sprinkle with 3/4 cup cheese, top with veggie mixture, and sprinkle with remaining 3/4 cup cheese. Bake until bubbling and cheese has just melted, 12 to 15 minutes. Let stand for about 5 minutes before serving.

Serves 6 to 8 as a side dish.

your mind is reeling and your heart is bleeding. But the end will be more satisfying than any we can dream up as we claim our sure legacy as children of God.

The One who makes all things new is still writing our stories. We have to remember that. Corrie ten Boom said, "Every experience God gives us, every person He puts in our lives, is the perfect preparation for the future that only He can see."[4] His eternal purpose for each and every one of us is at work, whether we consciously feel it or not. God often works silently behind the scenes, so the fact that we do not feel something proves nothing.

"I know the plans I have for you," says the Lord in Jeremiah 29:11. "*I know the plans.*" We miss that part sometimes when we read this verse. Only He knows the plans, and they are perfect for our lives. Sometimes we write our list and say to Him, *Here it is, Lord, make it happen!* And He says, *Just come alongside Me. I will take you to the greatest places.* Then God maneuvers us into bigger plans.

Our hope comes in believing that He is trustworthy and the Master Planner. Our past doesn't determine our future. God does! Nothing you've done or experienced can limit God or His power. Our histories do not determine our destinies any more than our current circumstances affect God's ability to keep His word. Our emotions don't reflect what's yet to come, and people can't control where we're headed. Only God determines our future, and you can count on Him to write your story in His own beautiful and extraordinary way.

This is what He says to you, to each of us, right now: *I hold your future in My hands. You can trust Me.*

Hopefully Ever After

Of course, trusting God with your future is even more difficult when you're not particularly thrilled with what He's doing in your present. Day to day, moment by moment, the challenges, disappointments, and difficulties of life can knock us back so hard that we lose our focus on the only true source of hope. Sometimes we start chasing after illusions, believing that lasting satisfaction would be ours if only we could grab hold of that elusive dream on which we've pinned our hopes.

When we base our hope on anything but Jesus, we may as well go ahead and check in at Heartbreak Hotel. So we urge you to consider this question, if you will:

On what have you based your hopes for this day, this year, this life? Think about it. Take a look at your life and your circumstances, the situations that God has placed you in at this moment. Are you living as if your hope will be met when you hit your weight goal? when you recover from illness? when you have enough money to retire? when you're finally blessed with a child or grandchild? when that special someone comes into your life at last?

Many women are pinning their hope on meeting a certain someone so their lives will finally begin. I (Kathy) have wrestled with that deep longing at different times in my life. Thankfully, I'm learning that life can be lived fully and richly even without a husband to share it with.

Don't get me wrong. I am human. I understand our desire and capacity to love and be loved, to share one's heart and mind and body. Sure, I go through moments of wanting to "belong" to someone. I feel the ache of wanting to be held ever so close. Like the tide, it washes over me on different days—a warm summer night, on Christmas, at the movie theater, or when I hear a romantic song. I've been known to have my teary moments.

But I don't wake up in the morning and say through my yawn, "Ohhh... I'm single..." I don't move through crowds with a sign on my back that reads S-I-N-G-L-E.

Yes, my singleness is a part of who I am but such a small part. Other people often seem more concerned about it than I am. One day my manager received a call: "Can Kathy write us a little article on being single?" Ugh. Such conversations always make me cringe just a bit. The "I can't believe you're still single" or "Why are you still single?" comments seem to buzz around me constantly. It's like an annoying fly in my car. I swat patiently until I can pull over and shoo it out my window.

At times like these I often think of Mary of Bethany sitting unashamedly at the feet of Jesus, lavishing Him with love and devotion. Can you imagine Jesus turning to her and saying, "Sweet daughter. My beloved. As much as you love Me, My words, My promises, and My love only apply if you get married. Otherwise you are so out of My plan. Sorry."

Or can you hear Jesus saying to His disciples, "Greater love has no one than this: to be married."

Of course not. That sounds crazy, doesn't it? But many people, including some singles, act as if that were His message.

Here are the true words of Jesus's heart: "Greater love has no one than this, that he lay down his life for his friends" (John 15:13). Our hope comes not in marriage, not in achieving our ideal weight, not in raising perfect children, not in having a healthy retirement portfolio, but in surrender, in laying down our lives—living with our hands and hearts open to God so that He can pour into them His treasures from heaven any time He desires.

What a life goal: for me to become small so that He can become big. The message I hear in these words is that being single doesn't mean I have to miss out on the passion and adventure of life. Sure, my body would love to feel a little passion. I am *not* in heaven, so I'll have longings and aches. I hate it sometimes. But it comes with the air I breathe, with being human. But, hey, He said I wouldn't lack any good thing (see Psalm 34:10), and I know what He means. Jesus keeps me satisfied and fulfilled.

As I keep surrendering my "losses," I gain the gifts of the lavishness of His love. My life possesses countless moments of joy. My relationships with my nieces are priceless. My friends' children bring delight to my soul. And my friends are glorious finds. Even without my parents, I have a true sense of family. My life is filled with loveliness and warmth. I deliberately choose to enjoy the romance of the moment, whether that means finding pleasure in an elegant meal, an engaging conversation, or the beauty of the ocean.

Singleness does not define me. Jesus does. My life is not on hold. I am not circling the airfield of life waiting to land in the arms of a man. I am flying, even if sometimes my wings feel a little bent. On days when my faith and hope are truly aligned, I am soaring, going higher places on earth as I humble myself toward heaven.

All for the Glory of Hope

God says that He will take us from glory to glory. "We all, with unveiled face, beholding as in a mirror the glory of the Lord, are being transformed into the same image from glory to glory" (2 Corinthians 3:18, NASB). This isn't simply a promise for past salvation or future fulfillment but for daily living. The Message says, "We are transfigured much like the Messiah, our lives gradually becoming brighter and more beautiful as God enters our lives and we become like him."

As the two of us examine our lives, we can see that this is true. There have been new days, new revelations, new opportunities, new ways of becoming more like Him. And even on those days when the big picture eludes us, when we yell and whine, He is patient to understand the depths of our cries. He knows we are fragile, and He knows we can only see in part. But "those who hope in the LORD will renew their strength" (Isaiah 40:31).

As we've already seen, the Spirit who raised Jesus from the dead lives in those who belong to Him (see Romans 8:11). That is true resurrection power. The One who rolled away the stone and defeated death is more than capable of working out His purposes in our lives today.

Sometimes, rather than releasing ourselves into God's care, we hide in the clefts of rocks, tucking ourselves away from all that we blame for our wounds. This may be true for you right now; you're reading this book in hiding. Of course, you come out to do the tasks of life, but you rush right back to your little cave, exhausted by the pain and disappointments that have come your way. Sometimes we just get so tired of swinging at life. We surrender to the hurt rather than to God, or we rant about the unfairness of our situation, and the pain only deepens.

Amy Carmichael wrote, "I think it must hurt the tender love of our Father when we press for reasons for His dealings with us, as though He were not Love, as though not He, but another chose our inheritance for us, and as though what He chose to allow could be less than the very best and dearest that Love Eternal had to give."[5]

Today you may be tempted to wonder why God is allowing your loved one to suffer a physical illness or permitting you yourself to suffer. Maybe you're feeling defeated in your ministry or career, wondering why you're not experiencing greater success. Maybe you question why He doesn't bring you a husband to meet the longings of your heart, or somehow intervene to improve your relationship with the husband you do have. Whatever your current circumstances, it's fairly certain that somewhere in your heart rustles a hope for some change, some healing, some fresh joy to fill your weary heart.

These days we have not only the stresses of our personal lives but the added stress and anxiety over events taking place nationally and globally. So many people awaken each day filled with fear about what is happening in the world. Amid the threats of terror, world peace seems more elusive than ever before. So where can we turn? Where can we find hope that brings peace even as the storms of life whirl threateningly all around us?

> *Chi cerca trova.*
> Who searches, finds.

In Psalm 62:5–6 David wrote, "Find rest, O my soul, in God alone; my hope comes from him. He alone is my rock and my salvation; he is my fortress, I will not be shaken." If we place our hope in anything or anyone other than God, we're going to be disappointed. We will always come up short and empty. The best-made plans change, circumstances change, and feelings change. There are always new seasons, new trials, and new circumstances. Even new *good* things can lead us to mistakenly place our hope in someone or something other than Christ, but inevitably such hopes will be dashed against the rocks of reality.

By contrast, when we, like David, turn to God as our refuge, we find rest and joy and unshakable peace. And the more often we do this, the more natural it will feel. If we allow Him to, He will enable us to walk strongly, even through the pain, and move onward with hope in our hearts. As Paul says to the Colossians,

As you learn more and more how God works, you will learn how to do *your* work. We pray that you'll have the strength to stick it out over the long haul—not the grim strength of gritting your teeth but the glory-strength God gives. It is strength that endures the unendurable and spills over into joy, thanking the Father who makes us strong enough to take part in every-thing bright and beautiful that he has for us. (Colossians 1:10–12, MSG)

God will give you "glory-strength" that spills joy over every moment of your day and enables you to face the unthinkable with hope. Life changes, but He never will. He is the constant. In an uncertain world, the constant certainty is Jesus. In that name, we find Hope.

Our prayer for you is like that of the apostle Paul: "May the God of hope fill you with all joy and peace as you trust in him, so that you may overflow with hope by the power of the Holy Spirit" (Romans 15:13).

Thoughts to *Noodle* On

1. If someone observed your words and actions today, where might they conclude your greatest hope lies? Why?

2. What does the name Jesus mean to you?

3. Describe one time when your hopes were dashed. How has that affected your ability to place your hope in Jesus?

4. Describe your biggest worry about the future. What steps will you take today to entrust that to God?

Chapter 5

Hope Never Leaves

Whatever challenges come your way, you don't have to face them alone

Do you remember *The Waltons*? In the television program, this big family—seven kids, plus parents and two grandparents—were all housed under one roof as they shared the messiness and joy of living in community: working together toward a goal, fighting and making up, celebrating the little victories of life even when times were lean. No matter where we grew up, the Waltons mirrored our own experience—"Goodnight, John-Boy"; "Goodnight, Vito"—because the television show powerfully captured the many aspects of life that get tangled up in relationships, especially with family!

As Italians with family trees that boast more branches than Starbucks has coffeehouses, both of us have a deep appreciation for family and all that it means. Yet we've also learned that relationships and human connections are all too fragile. Where deep love is present, deep pain often lurks nearby.

Like Ellie, I (Kathy) was born to first-generation Americans. My grandparents came over on the boat from Italy to Ellis Island, so my parents were born in

Brooklyn, as were my sister and I. We moved out to Long Island in the early sixties, and my childhood years were lived out next-door to my mother's two sisters, their families, and my maternal grandparents. The Espositos, Pellechias, Gallellis, and Troccolis formed our own little Italian commune! We ate together and played together and constantly got into one another's business together. Every Sunday, no matter whose table we gathered around, you could count on an abundance of macaroni, meatballs, and "gravy"—or as "Amerigans" call it, spaghetti sauce. Sunday gatherings also included generous portions of yelling and laughing and crying and

Ellie's Sensational Sauce

Yes, it cooks for hours, but I don't call this stuff liquid gold for nothing!

Ingredients

- 1/2 cup olive oil
- one or all of the following meats (see note below): 1 medium boneless loin of pork (can be shredded before serving), 1 pound sausage (sweet or spicy; can be sliced before serving), 1 pound meatballs (see meatball recipe on page 30)
- 1 medium sweet onion, finely chopped
- 2 (28-ounce) cans whole tomatoes (try to buy San Marzano canned tomatoes)
- 1 (6-ounce) can tomato paste mixed with 1 cup water
- 1/4 teaspoon pepper
- 1/4 teaspoon salt
- 1/2 tablespoon dry basil
- 1 tablespoon dry parsley
- 1/2 cup red wine (optional)

hugging. My cousins Carmine and Enrico were my bosom buddies until I started branching out in seventh grade and discovered life outside the family.

Yet even as my non-Italian friends introduced me to a broader perspective on the world, my heart remained tethered to home. My father held a particularly special place in my life as the one who encouraged my early efforts in music. I remember how, on the cusp of teenhood, I dreamed of being able to sing like Karen Carpenter, whose song "Close to You" was playing on the radio. Vocal artist Carole King also touched my adolescent soul with her perfect combination of lyrics,

- 2 tablespoons butter (optional)
- 1 teaspoon sugar (optional)

Cooking Instructions

1. Heat a deep pot or skillet over medium heat. Add olive oil to coat the bottom well. Brown all meat evenly in oil. (Don't overcook; meat will continue to cook in sauce.)
2. In another large pot, heat 1/4 cup olive oil. Add finely chopped onion and cook 5 minutes over medium heat, stirring.
3. One at a time, purée canned tomatoes (including liquid) in blender and add to onions. Add tomato paste mixed with 1 cup of water.
4. Add browned meat(s) to sauce pot. Add all other ingredients. (Add wine and/or water, if desired.) Cover and simmer on low heat for 3 to 4 hours, stirring to the bottom of the pot every 15 to 20 minutes. No time to stir? Brown meat, mix all ingredients in a Crockpot, and cook 4 hours on high.

Note: Recipe can easily be doubled or tripled. If you want to cook more than one kind of meat at a time, just brown each meat separately, then double or triple the other ingredients. Try to use all three meats. You can freeze the meat and the "gold" for a future feast.

melodies, and voice. I spent large portions of 1971 wearing out my copy of her album *Tapestry* as I played it and sang along for hours on end.

One day there was a knock at my bedroom door. "Kathleen, it's Daddy." As he stepped into my room he said, "I heard you singing. It sounds really good. Sing that again for me." Well, I sang again and haven't stopped singing since. Almost immediately I began singing in the choir and jazz band at school, and the journey prompted by my father's words of encouragement has taken me down some amazing roads.

Sadly, he didn't live long enough to see what his comments led to. When I was just fifteen, my father died of colon cancer. His absence left a huge hole in my family, in my heart, and in my life. It was a crucial age to lose a father. I would have loved to have had him around when I started dating and when I had to make some decisions that would affect my future and my career. Yet through this painful loss, as well as through the death of my mother in 1991, God has opened my eyes and my heart to hope, stepping in to fill the void with His love and grace.

Hope in a World of Hurt

Sooner or later, each of us will endure one of the most overwhelming heartaches we can suffer in this life: *being left*—whether through death, abandonment, or estrangement—by a husband, wife, child, father, sister, friend, or whomever. I (Kathy) remember when I was told that my mother had six months to live. Although I was thirty years old, I felt like a child soon to be orphaned. I was on the verge of losing the sense of security that comes from having a constant in your life, someone who on a daily basis cares if you are safe in this world. Although we may be surrounded by caring people, the death of any vital relationship leaves us feeling lost and vulnerable.

And even when all is well and we're enjoying the fruits of a loving relationship, something in our hearts longs for more. We ache for a deeper, more intimate connection. But when we pressure others to satisfy that yearning, we end up feeling more alone than ever.

The reality is that only One is capable of answering the longings of our hearts for constant connection and intimacy. Only One can truly say, "I will never leave you nor forsake you" (Joshua 1:5). (Even the best husbands and girlfriends need a break from us sometimes!)

So when the kids suddenly disappear at the mention of housecleaning, when your husband forgets your anniversary—again—or when no one seems to notice that you're staggering under the weight of life, you can turn toward the Hope who never walks away.

A Decidedly Unmagical Kingdom

I often talk about Logan, Jordan, and Jared—my dear friend Allyson's sons. Last fall I took the boys to Disney World. I was so excited to share this experience with them. The hotel we stayed in has three different sections, and I was careful to book our rooms in one of the sections closest to the cafeteria because I didn't want them to have to walk far.

We were eating breakfast one morning, and I told the boys, who were eleven, nine, and seven at the time, "Guys, I tried to bless you by being close to the cafeteria."

Jordan, the middle one, responded, "Yeah, that would have been really terrible to walk to the cafeteria!"

When I realized he wasn't kidding, I responded emphatically, "Jordan, there is nothing terrible about being at Disney World—nothing!"

At that moment Jared, the little one, said, "The only terrible thing is that we have to go home, and we can't stay here forever!"

I smiled because his statement touched me so. Even in my adulthood, I feel exactly like Jared. When I enter the Magic Kingdom and walk down Main Street USA, as I look off into the distance and catch sight of that white castle, I feel a touch of enchantment.

I want life to be like a walk through Disney. Playful, exciting, charming, and joyful, brimming with contentment and happy endings. But such moments are all too rare, aren't they?

Made for Another World

I believe that much of our dissatisfaction in this life stems from wanting what God originally intended for us to have in the Garden of Eden. We want peace and intimacy and joy. We could do without sorrow and struggle, without sin and shame. Most of us resonate with this comment from C. S. Lewis: "I find in myself a desire which no experience in this world can satisfy."

No experience in this world can satisfy our deepest desires. You know why? Lewis concluded, "The most probable explanation is that I was made for another world."[1]

We were made for another world! We're never going to feel quite comfortable here. Personally, I would love to come down hard on Eve for this, but the reality is that if we exchanged places, I would have had applesauce running down my chin.

So the fact remains that I am not in the garden, but my soul aches for it. Every part of my being yearns for it. I must continually remember that I was made for another world. We will no longer need faith or hope when we reach heaven. There, all will be known, realized, celebrated. Being "joyful and triumphant," as the Christmas carol says, will no longer be a seasonal concept but an eternal one. But during our stay here on earth we will have pain, and we will continue to have struggles.

In light of that reality listen to what God says in Hebrews 13:5: "Never will I leave you." In other words, we don't have to sit around longing for eternity or moaning over the Eden that *might* have been ours. No, we have hope here with us, right now. That shimmering truth outshines anything the Magic Kingdom has to offer.

Our hope comes from Jesus, who never abandons us. He is not going anywhere! He offers us His presence and power no matter how we feel, no matter what life brings, and no matter how many mistakes we make.

Hope Always Looks at Us Through Eyes of Love

I (Kathy) remember one weekend when I was speaking and singing at a Women of Faith conference. The group Avalon sang on Saturday, and as always they performed with amazing talent and energy. Two members of the group, Greg and Janna Long, are married, and I'm so happy they get to be together on the road.

On this particular weekend, Greg's mom had joined them, and she held their three-year-old daughter, Lilli, while the couple went on stage to perform. As Janna played the piano and sang and Greg joined the other members of the group in singing, I watched Lilli in her grandmother's arms. This dainty child, who has a face like a porcelain doll, stood up on her grandmother's lap and raised her little arms to wave as she shouted for her parents' attention. Janna and Greg were focused on the audience and their performance, and since the stage was set up in the round, it would have been nearly impossible for them to see their daughter's bid for attention. But some of us who weren't on stage at the moment couldn't help but stare at the precious sight of this excited and proud little one who wanted to be noticed by her mommy and daddy.

As I later reflected on that scene, I was struck by the thought that none of us ever have to jump up and down for the attention of the Lord. We are never far from His gaze. His eye is always on us.

Psalm 33:18 declares, "The eyes of the LORD are on those who fear him, on those whose hope is in his unfailing love." Often the thought of God watching us sparks a sense of fear or shame. *What must He think of me? I'm such a mess.*

But when God's gaze rests on you, He sees only that you are clothed with Christ (see Galatians 3:27), and His eyes are filled with love and compassion. He never looks at you with disdain for your bedhead or your runny mascara or your stained blouse. He never turns away in disgust because you've embarrassed Him with your weakness or your failures. No, His eyes are locked on you with delight:

> The LORD your God is with you,
>   he is mighty to save.
> He will take great delight in you,
>   he will quiet you with his love,
>   he will rejoice over you with singing. (Zephaniah 3:17)

What sweet reassurance to know the Lord is with you, taking delight in you and rejoicing over you.

When Jesus ascended into heaven, He said, "Surely I am with you always" (Matthew 28:20). Sometimes we forget His promise or find it hard to believe because we don't feel His loving gaze. You may be reading this and feeling forgotten by Him. But we know feelings aren't reliable. Feelings can flee and lie and taunt. What remains constant and unchanging, no matter our feelings or circumstances, is God's love for us.

I have learned that to avoid being sucked under by a tide of feelings, I have to move very quickly out of the emotional and into the rational and the spiritual.

When I see a wave of feelings headed my way, rather than letting it knock me off my feet, I ride it and let it carry me toward God. Some days I wake up and feel a mood coming on, a sadness. If I don't catch it—and sometimes I don't—I can drift into full-fledged depression, and my day is wasted in the dark. At such times I find it helpful to call to mind all that God has done in my life. I go through my mental Rolodex of events and moments where I've seen His hand at work. As I flip through scenes of His goodness, my heart moves from self-pity to thankfulness.

When it comes to hurtful situations involving other people, I make a practice of getting out of God's way by resisting the temptation to respond in the moment, whether it be in defense of myself or someone else. My goal is to give God room to work. I've witnessed the danger of sending angry e-mails or making confrontational phone calls before asking God to bring His sanity and wisdom to a situation. We often make things worse, and He always makes things better.

When we operate out of our emotions, we'll continually feel frail and tossed by the wind. But believing the promises of God and clinging firmly to Him will help us stand firm despite the fickleness of our feelings. On those days when life threatens to knock you off balance, center yourself in the hope that He is staying right by your side and rooting for you as you give Him your brokenness.

Remember, Jesus told His followers, "Are not five sparrows sold for two pennies? Yet not one of them is forgotten by God. Indeed, the very hairs of your head are all numbered. Don't be afraid; you are worth more than many sparrows" (Luke 12:6–7).

Feelings tend to blur our vision, causing us to lose sight of God's compassionate presence. But when you blink your spiritual eyes to clear away the fear and frustration and anger, you can gaze straight into the face of God and know that the look of love in His eyes has been there all along. You'll see signs of God's loving care all around you. He is so kind and faithful to always reassure us, whether through a word from a stranger, a call from a friend, or even just the sight of a bird outside your window serving as a quiet reminder that "His eye is on the sparrow, and I know He watches me."

Hope Never Leaves Us to Fend for Ourselves

Our always-present God not only gazes continually on us with love but also extends to us His strength. Contrary to the old saying "God helps those who help

Let's *Dish* About...
Signs of Hope

KT: You know, I have wrestled with my feelings so much in the course of my life. I'm talking major big-time matches, me versus the sumo "feelings" wrestler. Alone, I get pinned by my feelings every time. But when I let the Jesus in me fight the fight, that big ol' blob of emotions cowers like a little wimp.

Ellie, how do you stay centered on the hope we have in God?

EL: Believe it or not, I find reminders of hope in the morning headlines and the nightly news. Melting ice caps, genocide, HIV, school shootings, people being killed by family members. Such unsettling images confront my eyes and ears every day. And they send me back to the Bible, where I find comforting and deeply settling words to set my heart back on terra firma.

The Lord's ways are not always clear to me, but I find His constant love and His promise to always be with me soothing in these difficult, unpredictable times. He is Emmanuel, God with us. He is as close as our breath. He is the great Creator who is intricately involved with His creation. He is my Protector and Comforter. I will fear no evil.

KT: That seems like a healthy approach to the worries of the day. For me, the fact that Jesus rose from the dead is a cornerstone of my faith. The Resurrection brings my heart hope, because it reminds me that He can do anything. The impossible is nothing for God. I hold on to the promise that in His timing He can "move the stone" that is in front of any situation in my life.

❧

themselves," He doesn't wait to see what we can or will do in the face of a daunting challenge. Instead God comes to our aid when we are at our weakest point, least able to help ourselves.

In Isaiah 43:2 we read God's promise to His people:

When you pass through the waters,
    I will be with you;
and when you pass through the rivers,
    they will not sweep over you.
When you walk through the fire,
    you will not be burned;
    the flames will not set you ablaze.

What deep waters are you wading through today? What flames are licking at your heels? Are you in over your head with parenting a rebellious child? Are you overwhelmed by the challenge of caring for an aging parent? Are you drowning under the nonstop demands of life?

All of us face moments when it seems impossible even to put one foot in front of the other. Our natural instinct is to back away from the raging blaze of work, family, and ministry responsibilities, yet God not only calls us to go forward but also promises to walk alongside us.

When the Lord explained His plan to use Moses to lead the Israelites out of Egypt, the future leader of a nation expressed some intense insecurities and anxieties about being given that position. Talk about getting a serious stomachache. You've seen the nervous responses of would-be apprentices given tasks by Donald Trump. Now we're talking about receiving an assignment from the Maker of heaven and earth, the One who made the sun and put the stars in place! This was intimidation to the max, and Moses quaked in its grip. "Who am I, that I should go to Pharaoh and bring the Israelites out of Egypt?" (Exodus 3:11).

Can you relate to Moses's reluctance? At different times most of us have said,

- *I don't know if I can do this.*
- *I don't know if I can go through this.*
- *Am I capable of doing this, Lord?*

Sometimes God gives us a clear instruction, and we answer by saying we have to go and pray about it! Sometimes when I (Kathy) hear thunder, I picture God shaking His head back and forth from our responses to Him. Yet He tolerates all our questions patiently because He knows our humanity limits our ability to understand eternal plans. He also knows He will equip us and lead us through.

Listen to God's words of assurance to Moses: "Certainly I will be with you" (Exodus 3:12, NASB). How tender and reassuring of the Lord. He never leaves us to fend for ourselves.

> *Finché c'è vita c'è speranza.*
> ## While there's life, there's hope.

My (Ellie's) friend Monica has always been the picture of health. She is smart, petite, attractive, thin, fit, and did I mention she's a blonde? Monica is actually one of the three striking blondes who first responded ten years ago when I went door to door inviting neighbors to a Bible study. Always on the go and disciplined about exercise, Monica was at the local YMCA the morning she collapsed to the floor with unbearable pain in her head. She was rushed across the street to the Reston Hospital Center and was soon placed on a medevac helicopter to Georgetown University Hospital near Washington DC. One day and two invasive brain surgeries later, doctors concluded that Monica had suffered a massive cerebral aneurysm. She was left with paralysis of her left arm and leg, blurred vision, slurred speech, and a shaved head. Her prognosis was not hopeful.

Just a few months later, Monica was able to walk pretty swiftly with the help of a cane. Her vision and speech were normal, and she sported a funky rock-star hairdo. We all celebrated when she grew enough hair to warrant a bottle of blond color. Seven months after her hospitalization, she reapplied for her driver's license.

Both Monica and her dear husband, Mark, have witnessed an incredible outpouring of love throughout their ordeal. Their faith has been tested, tried, and found true. They have been purified in the fire of life's trials and come through stronger than ever in their determination to keep their eyes on God and not on circumstances. Monica expects full use of her arm and leg some day and presses on, knowing that God walks with her through every step she takes. When certain medical professionals share less-than-hopeful predictions, she reminds herself that they don't know the ways of the Great Physician. She remains hopeful, joyful, grateful, and unapologetic about expecting her miracle to come to full term. She knows that God will not leave her to fend for herself.

Whatever task you face, whatever trials loom ahead, you can hang your hope on the certainty that God will be right there alongside you, lending you His strength, His words, His power, and His peace.

You may say, "But I lost my husband." God says, *I will certainly be with you.*

You may be deep in depression or in the throes of an addiction. He says, *I will certainly be with you.*

"They just told me I have cancer." God says, *My beloved, I will certainly be with you.*

"Lord, my child is in such desperate trouble. I don't know what to do." God says, *I will certainly be with you.*

You see, no situation holds the power to make His promises null and void. It doesn't have to be well with your circumstances for it to be well with your soul.

In fact, Jesus openly declared, "In this world you will have trouble" (John 16:33). Not "you *may* have trouble" but "you *will* have trouble." We serve a God who never pulls any punches. He says what He means, and He means what He says. The reality is that life in this fallen, broken world will hurt sometimes. There's no getting around it.

But Jesus didn't stop there. Here's what He wants you to remember: "Take heart! I have overcome the world."

Take heart. Take hold of His heart. It is filled with all the hope you need to face each day with confidence and peace.

Hope Provides a Safe Haven for Your Heart

As we've seen, Jesus has promised to be with us always, but the concept of a reliable God can be difficult to wrap our minds around if we've been wounded in past relationships. We know countless women whose fathers or husbands have been anything but reflections of Christ. Other women have waited an agonizingly long time for just the right man to come along, then finally risked their hearts, only to be wounded beyond imagination. And how many mothers bear emotional scars because a child has rejected their love and closed off communication?

So many of us retreat emotionally in the wake of feeling abandoned. We run and hide, attempting to encase our hearts in a protective covering that will numb our pain.

I (Kathy) have definitely done this at different points in my life. I've lived through severe depression, and I suffered with bulimia for ten years. Bulimia is a nasty food addiction, and it can go on for years without people's knowing the ugly truth. When I was on tour with Michael W. Smith in the early eighties, my gift of singing was intact, but I was a mess. Often I would literally curl up in a ball when I got home from a performance, hating myself, hating life, and feeling like the biggest fraud.

But hiding is an enemy of healing. We must reveal ourselves and our wounds if we are to be healed. I needed to entrust my heart to God's care so He could get to the truth of what lay inside the deepest parts of me. Why was I doing this? I needed to unravel the web of pain and sorrows, the tangle of questions, anger, and doubts. He gently peeled away my pain, layer by layer, exposing the darkness of my spirit to His glorious light.

Yet even after my bulimia was under control, I still suffered under the weight of depression, struggling some days just to get out of bed. Maybe you know exactly what I'm talking about. In truth God was right there all the time, just as He is with you, offering me the safe shelter of His arms. But I spent so much time looking over my shoulder at the fear and pain chasing me that on many days I completely passed Him by.

During all those years of suffering and fighting depression, I had no idea that I had a serotonin problem. I will never forget when my dear friends Ellie and Allyson spoke to me about my mood swings: "We think you have a problem."

"What do you mean?" I asked defensively. "What kind of problem?"

"We think you have some kind of imbalance. You've been going from highs to lows for years. It's got to stop. We think you need medication."

Ugh. That nasty word. I'm sorry to say that it triggered in me a sense of shame. But I've learned the hard way about the importance of humbling ourselves and remaining teachable throughout this life, because God can't do anything with us if we keep our hearts closed down. So I finally sought help from a professional who prescribed a low dosage of medication. Before long, the fog started to clear, and I finally was able to recognize God's presence and enter into the hope and safety He offered.

Ellie now jokingly insists that I misinterpreted her advice to try "prayer and meditation," *not* medication! But we both realize that in certain situations no amount of talking can lift someone out of depression. Sometimes people truly need medication. Yes, they need the Word. Yes, they need the spiritual strength and hope that comes only by God's presence. But as my situation confirmed, sometimes there also is a physiological need.

As I look back through those seasons that held such incredible heartache for me, I see more clearly than ever how faithful God was to stay close. I'm indescribably thankful for the truth of the gospel, which reveals that God loves me just as I am and not just as I will be. In the midst of my weakness and frailty, He has sheltered me. He has been my covering and my hero. He has never left me. And each day in various ways He whispered these words to my soul: "I have made you and I will carry you; I will sustain you and I will rescue you" (Isaiah 46:4).

Billy Graham wrote about the paradoxical blessing wrapped up in our difficult days: "In the midst of trials we can thank God because we know he has promised to be with us, and he will help us. We know that he can use times of suffering to draw us closer to himself."[2]

Sometimes when we are hurting, we want what *we* consider the miraculous. *Part the Red Sea, Lord! Rain manna from heaven! I could use a little Old Testament action right about now.* Yet most times He comes inconspicuously, as He did to the woman at the well. He reassures us that He knows all about our situations and us. He knows how tired we are. He knows how much shame and guilt and fear we carry in our hearts every day. The past, the present, and the future can hold all sorts of emotions and stress. He knows we need reassurance that all will be well. So He speaks words of hope. But many times we miss His gentle voice because we are listening for thunder.

As I look back to the times when I felt God carry me or rescue me, I realize He has often done so in small, gentle ways that have had powerful effects on my life's course. I will hear a lyric of a song that I am convinced an angel was sent to sing to me. I will receive a card in the mail that might have two sentences of encouragement in it, and I know God guided the hand that wrote it just for me.

One of my heroes of the faith is David, whose life story and psalms reveal a man who understood the depths of despair and the heights of hope. He knew the pain of betrayal from his mentor Saul, from his wife Michal, and from his own son Absalom. He knew the fear of being hunted, the sorrow of confronting his own sin, and the hope of God's faithfulness that carried him through it all. David wrote in Psalm 62:

> God, the one and only—
>> I'll wait as long as he says.
> Everything I need comes from him,
>> so why not?
> He's solid rock under my feet,
>> breathing room for my soul,
> An impregnable castle:
>> I'm set for life....
>
> My help and glory are in God
>> —granite-strength and safe-harbor-God—
> So trust him absolutely, people;
>> lay your lives on the line for him.
>> God is a safe place to be. (verses 1–2, 7–8, MSG)

God is a safe place to be. This reminds me of that scene from *The Wizard of Oz* when Dorothy woke up from her dream in her bed in Kansas and immediately knew she was in a place of comfort and safety. Looking at her loved ones, she cried, "There's no place like home!" God is my heart's home. Like David, I will "trust him absolutely." There's no place like Jesus.

Hope Never Walks Away, No Matter What

Have you ever wondered why it is that God so often repeats His promises: "I will be with you. Never will I leave you; never will I forsake you"? Could it be that He knows how difficult it is for us to remember that truth when our faith smacks up against reality?

The truth of God's unshakable love is hard to grasp in this world where people betray us or walk away or unintentionally let us down. We all hurt one another. We all fall short in relationships. So often our love comes with conditions, with strings attached. Out of pain and pride and bitterness and even shame caused by our own mistakes, how often have we walked away, leaving relational casualties in our wakes?

By contrast—gorgeous, stunning contrast—God's love is everlasting, and His hand is always outstretched to selflessly give to us an abundance of hope. Nothing shocks Him. Nothing has ever "occurred" to God. He already knows! And the most wonderful thing is that we can't out-sin the love He has in His heart for us.

His is not a just-as-long-as-you-make-me-happy commitment. He says, "*Never* will I leave you!" He doesn't emotionally and physically check out when we mess up. He doesn't slam the door, leaving us to wonder when He will be back.

Sometimes, though, *we* walk away from hope. Just as in our human relationships, we allow our pain and pride and bitterness and shame to chase us into hiding. We sever our connection with God because we just don't think we can face Him, or we close Him out with walls of anger.

Look at what happened with Adam and Eve. They sinned and then hid. God said, "Where are you?" Of course, He knew exactly where they were; He was really asking Adam and Eve, "Where are you in relation to Me?"

The purpose of the stories in Scripture are not to tell us what God did. Their purpose is to tell us what God *does*. Thousands of years later He still asks us, "Where are you in your relationship with Me?"

He wants an answer from each of us not for His own sake but to help us honestly evaluate what we believe about God and where we stand when it comes to trusting Him.

In those times when we fail to trust, when we let go of hope, even then God doesn't let go of us. Author Jerry Bridges compares our heavenly Father's protective, continual presence to that of a parent who firmly grips a child's hand to prevent her from running into the street or getting lost in a crowd: "That's a picture of God's way with us. He is pleased when we cling to His hand, so to speak, in dependence on Him. But whether we cling to Him or not, He grips our hand. As David said, 'Your right hand will hold me fast' (Psalm 139:10)."[3]

Hope Delights in Giving Unexpected Gifts

Like a loving father, God continually surprises us with His generosity. "If you then, being evil, know how to give good gifts to your children, how much more will your Father who is in heaven give what is good to those who ask Him!" (Matthew 7:11, NASB).

At times we fail to recognize His gifts, because we were looking for something else. We say things like, "Well, she has gotten this, and I've only gotten that." Or, "Why did You allow that to happen for her and not for me?" Our complaining and pouting cloud the hope that God has a specific plan for us. What we are really doing in those instances is accusing Him of forgetting about us, when the truth is that He is working out everything for our good.

In God's economy timing is everything. And it is perfect. I (Kathy) never could have done in my twenties or even my early thirties the kind of ministry I am doing now in my fifties. It is as if God was waiting for my heart to catch up with my testimony. Our testimonies not only shape us and grow our hearts to trust Him more, but they also give us the ability to offer others hope and wisdom and comfort. The times we squirm beneath God's steady hand of mercy are the very times He uses in our futures to show His glory.

God continues to say, "I will be with you, always." He will uniquely write your story every single day until you meet Him face to face. The surprises He weaves into the pages of your life will be better than your well-laid plans and highest dreams, more incredible than fairy tales. God says, "I am writing your chapters; just wait on Me, and see My glory."

I (Kathy) am determined never to get caught up in moaning about the absence of a husband or children, because I want to revel in the amazing and unique ways God has placed me within the family of His divine choosing. I love and cherish Ellie's three children and Allyson's three children and my sweet nieces, Maria and Gina. They are all so precious to me.

Two years ago I had the joy of seeing Ellie's son Jordan perform in his high-school musical. I've known this kid since he was two years old. Now he's practically grown up: handsome, big, and strong. He has Fred Flintstone toes. But he's more Renaissance man than cave man. Besides being a football player, he participates in theater and singing groups.

So there I was in the high-school auditorium with the family—Ellie proudly taking photos, Capri (his then thirteen-year-old sister) seemingly bored, Grandma grinning broadly. And I sat there, tears welling up in my eyes before he even sang or danced. Something about his choosing to be in the play really got to me, this strong and brilliant kid who is so kind. I am so thankful for young men like him in this world—in my world.

God knows exactly what I need, and He has given me a richer life than I ever dreamed of. Soul rich. Heart rich. People rich. He is truly a keeper of promises, and rather than clenching my fists around my own dreams, I want to open my hands to receive whatever gifts He chooses to give me. Every time I do, He fills them to overflowing with evidence of His love, with undeniable proof that Hope never leaves.

Thoughts to *Noodle* On

1. Have you ever experienced the loss of a close relationship? How has that experience affected your approach to other relationships? your view of God?

2. Describe a difficult time in which you found hope in God's presence. What evidence did you have that He was walking alongside you?

3. If God were to ask you, *Where are you in your relationship with Me?* what would your answer be?

4. As you think about the truth that "God is a safe place to be," what dream, struggle, or disappointment can you entrust to His care today?

Chapter 6

Hold On to Hope

Are you grasping at illusions or clinging to the hand of God?

I (Ellie) remember Nonna's kitchen with great fondness and longing. She is the one to thank (or blame) for my high standards when I dine in Italian restaurants, because everything she created was *tutto delizioso*. Even 7Up tasted better in her kitchen than anywhere else. She is the one who coaxed me to eat *pasta e fagioli* (pasta and beans), *carciofi* (artichokes), and *vongole al olio* (clams with olive oil on linguine). She also fed me *fiori di zucca* (the flower from the zucchini). She dipped it in egg and flour and deep-fried those bright orange blossoms to a golden brown delicacy. Mmmmm.

Nonna is also to blame (or thank) for my cluelessness in the preparation of all things *Italiano*. She lived nearby for almost forty years of my life. Why struggle with a recipe and mess up the kitchen if I could stop over at Nonna's? In her later years she was delighted whenever I called to ask if I could bring my three bambinos over for *pastina e pane* (essentially soup and bread).

Nonna had a magic touch when it came to creating main dishes, side dishes, desserts, snacks, and appetizers from little more than flour, eggs, and yeast. Just one taste of her made-from-scratch pastas, pizzas, breads, calzones, and *zeppoli* sent me into raptures of joy, ecstasy, surrender, and a general feeling of, "If I die right now, life is good."

Nonna grew up in northern Italy, so she did not fit the stereotype for Italian grandmothers with her shy personality, humble presence, lovely gentleness, and yes, even a style of food preparation that was atypical, since most people are familiar primarily with classic southern Italian fare.

I've read that the sense of smell is quite powerful in stirring memories, and I know this to be true. Once a year or so, a very particular aroma will intersect my discerning nostrils, and I'll close my eyes, feel my heartbeat slow, sigh a deep sigh, wipe away a tear—and yearn to be back in Nonna's kitchen.

Running on Empty

Thinking back to how Nonna's incomparable cooking filled me with a sense of satisfaction and joy brings to mind the ever-present hope we have in Jesus that should fill our souls to overflowing. And yet how often do we find ourselves running on empty rather than feasting at the sumptuous banquet God has prepared for His children?

First Kings 19:1–15 tells a story about the prophet Elijah. He had become a constant thorn in the side of Queen Jezebel, who was absolutely enraged by his refusal to go along with the false prophets who spoke the words she wanted to hear. Elijah spoke only the words of God Almighty, and the Lord had done many miracles for him and through him. Yet at this point in the story, we find Elijah running into the desert after Jezebel had threatened his life. Despite all his past successes, the prophet was completely drained of hope. He felt depressed and abandoned:

> Elijah was afraid and ran for his life. When he came to Beersheba in
> Judah, he left his servant there, while he himself went a day's journey
> into the desert. He came to a broom tree, sat down under it and prayed
> that he might die. (verses 3–4)

Elijah's actual words were, "I have had enough, LORD. Take my life."

Nonna Tina's Pastina

For cold days, rainy days, old-movie days, good-book days, and when-you-miss-your-Grandma days—pastina is the ultimate bowl of comfort. *Mangia!*

Ingredients

- 6 cups water, plus 1 tablespoon
- 2 large chicken bouillon cubes (we recommend Knorr) or 5 to 6 small ones
- 8 tablespoons butter (1 stick)
- 1 (12-ounce) box pastina, or tiny stars (acini de pepe or orzo will do)
- 2 eggs
- grated cheese to sprinkle
- salt and pepper to taste

Cooking Instructions

1. Bring 6 cups water to boil in a medium pot. Add bouillon cubes and butter; stir 1 minute.
2. Add pastina, lower heat, and cook until water is mostly absorbed, stirring often. When it has almost a porridge consistency, remove from heat.
3. Whisk 2 eggs with a tablespoon of cold water in small bowl. Slowly pour eggs into pastina, stirring vigorously and scraping the bottom of the pot. If it is too hot, dry, or thick, add a splash of milk or water.
4. Serve in bowls and sprinkle liberally with grated cheese. Watch it disappear.

Serves 6.

I have had enough, Lord. Can you relate to that sense of being utterly over-whelmed by life? What woman hasn't reached a point of complete exhaustion with arbitrating sibling squabbles or navigating office politics or struggling uphill against an avalanche of dirty laundry? Or worse, fighting off the nausea from chemo or radiation treatments, wrestling against depression, or working two jobs in a desperate effort to make ends meet?

I have had enough, Lord could aptly describe how many of us feel on any given day. And like Elijah, we want nothing more than to flop ourselves down under a tree (or on the couch) and fall asleep. Here's what happened next to our weary prophet:

> All at once an angel touched him and said, "Get up and eat." He looked
> around, and there by his head was a cake of bread baked over hot coals, and
> a jar of water. He ate and drank and then lay down again.
>
> The angel of the LORD came back a second time and touched him and
> said, "Get up and eat, for the journey is too much for you." So he got up
> and ate and drank. (verses 5–8)

Is it just us, or does all this eating and drinking prompt you to wonder if Elijah was Italian?

Seriously, it's clear from this passage that God knew exactly what Elijah needed. In keeping with the promises we saw in the previous chapter, our heavenly Father didn't leave Elijah to fend for himself. Recognizing that the journey was too much, He provided a safe haven where the prophet could regain his physical strength and emotional stability.

In the same way, God provides for us when our reserves are exhausted. But like Elijah, we have to choose to get up and partake of what God offers. Then we can tackle the next stage of our journey:

> Strengthened by that food, he traveled forty days and forty nights until he
> reached Horeb, the mountain of God. There he went into a cave and spent
> the night.
>
> And the word of the LORD came to him: "What are you doing here,
> Elijah?" (verses 8–9)

At first that sounds like a strange question for our all-knowing God to pose; it seems pretty obvious what Elijah is doing: putting as much distance as possible between himself and the Queen of Mean. But as we've seen before, God's questions are more for us than for Him. Maybe this was His way of prompting Elijah to seriously consider what his choices revealed about the state of his faith.

> He replied, "I have been very zealous for the LORD God Almighty. The Israelites have rejected your covenant, broken down your altars, and put your prophets to death with the sword. I am the only one left, and now they are trying to kill me too." (verse 10)

Can you hear the discouragement in his voice? Despite all he has seen of God's provision and power, at this moment Elijah cannot hear anything but Jezebel's shrill threats echoing in his mind.

But instead of scolding the prophet for his lack of faith, God sends him out of the cave and into the light:

> The LORD said, "Go out and stand on the mountain in the presence of the LORD, for the LORD is about to pass by."
>
> Then a great and powerful wind tore the mountains apart and shattered the rocks before the LORD, but the LORD was not in the wind. After the wind there was an earthquake, but the LORD was not in the earthquake. After the earthquake came a fire, but the LORD was not in the fire. And after the fire came a gentle whisper. When Elijah heard it, he pulled his cloak over his face and went out and stood at the mouth of the cave.
>
> Then a voice said to him, "What are you doing here, Elijah?" (verses 11–13)

Whispering Hope

Just like Elijah, we often speak to God out of our disappointment and sorrow, reminding Him of what we have done: *How could You let this happen, Lord? Don't You remember how faithfully I've served You?*

Instead of scolding us for our pride or raging about our lack of faith, God gently responds, *I'm right here with you in the midst of the storm. Are you going to listen to the world around you, or will you let My voice bring you comfort and be your guide?*

God came to Elijah in a gentle whisper. Not in the wind. Not in the earthquake. Not in the fire. He came in a gentle whisper after the spectacular happened. In our culture we have become addicted to the spectacular. We are looking for the greatest high from God rather than seeking the great God on high. Yet more often than not, God speaks in a gentle whisper.

Let's *Dish* About...
Filtering Out the Noise

EL: What are some things that make it harder for you to hear the voice of Hope?

KT: I find it hard to hear the voice of Hope when I face situations that *I* have labeled impossible. It could be anything from hearing someone has been diagnosed with a fourth-stage cancer to reading about unrest in the Middle East. Such news zaps my spiritual and emotional energy until I place my hope on the promises of God and rearrange my heart to find peace and refocus my mind on eternal perspectives. Then I can hear the truth that nothing is impossible with God.

EL: It seems that difficult circumstances—whether they be financial, physical, social, professional, marital, emotional, or whatever—have a way of flooding our thoughts and drowning out the voice of Hope.

So in the middle of all the insanity of life, how do we stay in a position to hear God's voice? How do we hold on to hope when our days are busy and filled with all kinds of stress? We are bogged down in the details while life rushes past. Hold on to hope? It's all we can do just to hold on! How can we be sure we'll hear God's gentle whisper of hope?

I (Kathy) would like to suggest a word picture to illustrate both the problem and the solution: in the world of music recording, noise-floor levels are extremely important. Noise floors are simply the level of all the sounds around you in a

Pain at any level tends to demand our attention, drain our energy, and darken our outlook. Everything about life is impacted when we are in pain.

KT: That is so true.

EL: Yet as you've pointed out, Kathy, God is the essence of hope through every trial we encounter in this life. I know that to be true both intellectually and experientially, but I occasionally get lost in the fog of pain. Did God move away? Is He playing hide-and-seek? No, that's not His way. The problem is my own tendency to wander during times of pain. I want to fix things, to have instant relief, to effect change on my terms. When I'm busy trying to be my own savior, I lose sight of where my hope truly comes from.

Lifeguards, firefighters, and counselors will tell you that it is impossible to save people who try to save themselves. We must all admit our need for a Savior. Then we can hear the voice of Hope saying, "Let Me lead you to safety."

particular place at a particular time, things like coughing or snoring or breathing. For example, in a crowded restaurant you may find yourself talking louder than normal because the noise floor in the restaurant is higher than in your living room (unless you have small kids at home).

In a recording studio, the noise floor can be increased by any number of things, including the sound equipment itself. Obviously, even at a low level such noises can affect the quality of the recording. I was in the studio cutting my last album when, in the middle of singing a quiet ballad, I heard a loud grinding noise in my earphones. I told the engineer, who investigated the source of the noise. He discovered that a bus parked outside the studio had been left running.

Just as the noise of that bus drowned out the words I was singing and distracted me from the task at hand, the noise of our lives can drown out God's quiet whisper of hope. We're bombarded with noise from all kinds of things—from entertainment, from the media, from our culture, from the demands of relationships and work and the other forms of stress our days hold. That's why we all need to lower the noise-floor levels in our lives.

God is subtle enough that we won't hear Him unless we make the effort, yet He is obvious enough that we can't miss His voice when our ears are attuned to it. So we must find ways to lower the hubbub of our existence. The solution to accomplishing that will be different for each of us. Only you know what needs to go. Only you know what needs to change to take the level down a bit. But we'd like to offer a few suggestions for how you can turn off some of the meaningless clatter and tune in more clearly to the voice of Hope.

What Goes In Must Come Out

What we feed into our minds and hearts significantly impacts our spiritual health, but are we as conscious as we should be about what we fill our souls with during the course of a day? Some of us pray, *God, will You please lift me up?* or, *Lord, make me Your woman,* then spend our days spoon-feeding our souls on garbage in the form of trashy novels or magazines. Others pack in the equivalent of spiritual junk food by watching shows centered on the seamy side of life, then wonder why they feel weighed down by worry and despair.

One of the things I (Kathy) have learned to do through my struggles with depression is to choose carefully what I put into my mind. I refuse to read certain books or watch certain television shows or movies that I know will leave an imprint on my spirit. Lately I also have been challenging myself about how much I watch the news. As I view the negative coverage of events in our world, I sometimes find myself feeling defeated or angry, and it makes me want to crawl in a hole somewhere. Of course, I believe God reigns sovereign over it all, but spending too much time watching the news distracts my attention from what He has already done and is currently doing.

The apostle Paul wrote, "Finally, brothers, whatever is true, whatever is noble, whatever is right, whatever is pure, whatever is lovely, whatever is admirable—if anything is excellent or praiseworthy—think about such things" (Philippians 4:8). How wise we would be to follow that advice, to screen out the noises of life by filtering them through that grid.

In addition to being selective about the words and images I feed into my mind, I choose carefully whom I spend my time with, because conversations and opinions affect the way I feel. The words seep right into my heart, into my psyche, into my mind.

Remember our weary prophet? When God came in a gentle whisper and asked for the second time, "What are you doing here, Elijah?" the man gave the same reply as before:

I have been very zealous for the LORD God Almighty. The Israelites have rejected your covenant, broken down your altars, and put your prophets to death with the sword. I am the only one left, and now they are trying to kill me too. (1 Kings 19:14)

For so long, Elijah had heard only negative words from everyone around him. The constant barrage of criticism and rejection left him feeling isolated. So God suggested he get some new friends:

Go back the way you came, and go to the Desert of Damascus. When you get there, anoint Hazael king over Aram. Also, anoint Jehu son of Nimshi king over Israel, and anoint Elisha son of Shaphat from Abel Meholah to succeed you as prophet. Jehu will put to death any who escape the sword of Hazael, and Elisha will put to death any who escape the sword of Jehu. Yet I reserve seven thousand in Israel—all whose knees have not bowed down to Baal and all whose mouths have not kissed him. (verses 15–18)

The Lord not too subtly pointed out that, far from being "the only one left," Elijah was one of seven thousand who remained faithful to the one true God. And in addition to directing Elijah to anoint two new kings, God gave him a co-worker in the battle for truth, Elisha.

The people we allow to have voices in our lives exert a vital influence over what we believe and how we will live. Each of us is stronger when we're surrounded by people who are willing to say, "That is unacceptable," or, "You need to look at this." We need that sort of iron-sharpens-iron friendship. In addition, we need people whose words lift us up rather than drag us down. Proverbs 12:25 says, "Anxiety in a man's heart weighs it down, but a good word makes it glad" (NASB). Who are your intimates, and how do they contribute to the levels of hope in your life?

We need to surround ourselves with hope-filled people and put ourselves in places where God can breathe His life into us. When we do, when we allow the Holy Spirit to light His fire under the dried-up kernels of our lives: *Pop! Pop! Pop!* Faith! Healing! Comfort! Hope! All these burst forth to fill our hearts.

Do you want to see your spirit bounce up? Get around good words, whether from people or books or the Word of God itself.

The Power of Praise

Of course, our hope is renewed not only by receiving good words but by speaking them as well.

Recently I (Kathy) went through some boxes in the attic. While perusing old photographs, cards, and letters, I came across a box of cassette tapes. Some were interviews I've kept through the years, and some were sermons I had accumulated for my "I will listen to this someday" collection.

One caught my eye. The label read *1986—Belmont Church.* The sermon heading was simply "Pride." I was a member of Belmont Church when I lived in Nashville years ago, and I have visited that thriving body a few times in my recent move back to the South. I couldn't recall what might have prompted me to keep a recording of this particular service, but I figured it had to be good because I don't save many. So I went into my office closet to retrieve one of those now-ancient cassette players, popped in the tape, and sat down to give it a listen.

Much to my surprise, I heard myself at twenty-eight years old reciting Psalm 34. Like a refreshing spray of water on a Tennessee summer day, the sound of my voice took me back to a precious encounter with God, a sweet reminder of a time when He watered my barren spirit with the Word so that hope could bloom once again.

Back then, I was getting ready to go on tour with Michael W. Smith. As I mentioned before, at that time I was struggling with bulimia and depression and several other unresolved issues. That particular Sunday morning I was determined not to go to church. Lifting my body out of bed seemed too much of a chore, let alone sitting in a pew for an hour.

But my friend Allyson, who was my roommate at the time, firmly encouraged me to go. I decided to get up and get dressed, but I felt as if I were reporting for duty in a sleepwalk. We got to church and found seats. The sound of all those happy voices singing and praising only increased my misery, and I yearned for the service to be over.

I reached for Allyson's Bible, which was resting between us, and opened it to Psalm 34. In those difficult days, that passage served as a consistent anchor through the raging storms of emotion. I particularly drew hope from verse 18, which declares, "The LORD is close to the brokenhearted and saves those who are crushed in spirit." I couldn't think of any words that better described me, and I was buoyed by the thought that my distress itself qualified me for the grace of His presence.

That day in church, as I buried myself in the psalm to shut out the happy people, I heard God speak to my spirit: *I want you to read Psalm 34 before the congregation.*

I dismissed it as if a gnat flew by.

I want you to read Psalm 34 before the congregation.

You can't be serious, God. You know how I feel. You know where I am...

And still the gentle voice spoke persistently to my spirit.

I sat there for a minute and then did what any good trusting Christian would do. I asked God to give me a sign if He really meant it. (Don't tell me you wouldn't do the same!)

And at that very moment the worship leader said this to the congregation: "Let's speak God's Word to one another."

A chill went up my spine. I had asked for a sign, and He answered me. Even in my sorry shape, I knew that didn't leave me much wiggle room. So as people started to call out different words and phrases from the Scriptures, I slowly made my way to the front of the church and stood behind the podium.

My hands shook, and the sound of my voice speaking, personalizing David's words, startled me.

> I will extol the LORD at all times;
>> his praise will always be on my lips.
> My soul will boast in the LORD;
>> let the afflicted hear and rejoice.
> Glorify the LORD with me;
>> let us exalt his name together.
>
> I sought the LORD, and he answered me;
>> he delivered me from all my fears.
> Those who look to him are radiant;
>> their faces are never covered with shame.
> This poor woman called, and the LORD heard me;
>> he saved me out of all my troubles...

As I read, those words began to wash clear the eyes of my heart. About halfway through, at the very spot that had so often brought me comfort, my voice started to crack, and I began to cry. But out of obedience I continued to speak those words of praise, words overflowing with hope:

The righteous cry out, and the LORD hears them;
    he delivers them from all their troubles.
The LORD is close to the brokenhearted
    and saves those who are crushed in spirit.

A righteous man may have many troubles,
    but the LORD delivers him from them all;
he protects all his bones,
    not one of them will be broken.

Decades later as I listened to that recording, I marveled anew at the tender touch of God and the power of praise. The Lord wanted me to firmly put my stake in the ground that day, to declare before Him and before His people the truth of the hope I have in Him. He wanted those words to go deep into my marrow.

> *Cuor forte rompe cattiva sorte.*
> **Nothing is impossible to a willing heart.**

That Sunday wasn't the only time I have been around people who were wholeheartedly and joyfully worshiping God while I listened in silence. On more occasions than I can count, other people's words of praise have fallen all around me like moonlight, shining warmth and hope into the darkness of my emotional prison. As I listen to others worship, I find myself starting to mouth words, then whisper, and then praise as I open up and start talking to Him again.

The prisons we build for ourselves may shut us in, but they cannot shut God out. Praise somehow penetrates and pierces through passages that have been walled up. It reminds me of what happened when Paul and Silas were thrown into prison by the Romans:

About midnight Paul and Silas were praying and singing hymns to God,
and the other prisoners were listening to them. Suddenly there was such a
violent earthquake that the foundations of the prison were shaken. At once

all the prison doors flew open, and everybody's chains came loose. (Acts 16:25–26)

Thank God, the praises of His people can unlock the chains of loneliness and sorrow. Every word breaks a link as we are reminded of all that He is and all that He is able to do, and we're able to once more take the hand of hope that He extends.

I will praise you forever for what you have done;
>   In your name I will hope, for your name is good.
>   I will praise you in the presence of your saints. (Psalm 52:9)

Whenever I step out on a platform to sing or speak of the faithfulness of God, I am always aware that each word of praise is also pouring into my own soul. As I later talk with people at the book table, they grace me with encouraging comments about what the Lord did for them through my song. I smile, as I know that the same thing happened for me.

Prayers Don't Have to Be Pretty

One of the reasons the two of us love the psalms is that David was so honest and vulnerable in his writings. We Italians aren't big on stuffing our emotions, so we relate to his full range of feelings. He was sometimes elated, sometimes contrite. He cried out to God through every season of his life. He sang God's praises, and he begged God for mercy. You never have to guess how David was feeling.

So often, Christians put up appearances that all is well. David didn't do that. He poured out his heart to God, and God honored him for it. He continually brought himself into the presence of God, and it didn't go unnoticed in the heavenlies. God described David as "a man after his own heart" (1 Samuel 13:14).

David wrote of the Lord, "I hold on to you for dear life, and you hold me steady as a post" (Psalm 63:8, MSG). What a great visual! At times all of us feel as if we're being tossed by the winds of life, pulled toward a vortex of overcommitment or anxiety or illness. Yet God remains constant and immovable. Another psalmist wrote: "Your love stands firm forever…you established your faithfulness in heaven itself" (Psalm 89:2). When we feel buffeted by life, how comforting to know that we can take hold of Hope and He will keep us steady.

As Luis Palau wrote, "Prayer must be our first line of defense, not a last resort."[1]

Even when you feel too cast down or overwhelmed to even utter a prayer, you can simply say, "Help me, God." *That* is holding on to Hope. As huge as our God is, He doesn't need a huge prayer. He doesn't need a lavish prayer. He just needs an open heart so He can pour in His hope and peace.

History Lessons

Interestingly, the psalms reveal that David not only conversed freely with God but also talked to himself on more than one occasion. This is a bit different from those of us who talk to ourselves in the produce aisle of the grocery story. David's conversations with himself aren't of the "oh yeah, I need some garlic" kind; he was addressing his soul, reminding himself of the things he knew to be true about God:

> Why are you down in the dumps, dear soul?
>> Why are you crying the blues?
> Fix my eyes on God—
>> soon I'll be praising again.
> He puts a smile on my face.
>> He's my God.
> When my soul is in the dumps, I rehearse
>> everything I know of you. (Psalm 42:5–6, MSG)

Present circumstances can cause us to lose sight of all the past occasions when God has come through for us. The Enemy of our souls wants to twist our perspective, leading us to believe his lies that we are insignificant and that God is negligent.

Yet Deuteronomy 7:9 tells us, "Know therefore that the LORD your God is God; he is the faithful God, keeping his covenant of love to a thousand generations of those who love him and keep his commands." When we grab hold of what we know to be true about God, He has a way of bursting through Satan's lies to reveal what really matters: we will make it through because our Lord will never abandon us.

This is why it's vital to continually rehearse the stories of God's past faithfulness, both to us and to others. Looking back through history reminds us to keep our eyes on God, not on our circumstances. Had these people based their responses solely on what they could see rather than on what God could do...

- Noah would have tossed aside God's blueprint for the ark.
- Abraham would have given up hope for a baby boy.
- David would never have fought the big guy.
- Daniel surely would have been lunch.
- Joshua would never have thought to twist and shout.
- Nehemiah would have stopped making mud pies.
- Mary would not have cooperated with the angel.
- The disciples would have sent the crowds away to find their own sushi sandwiches.
- Jesus might have been tempted to cancel the Last Supper.

Each of these people was well aware of the major storm clouds hovering overhead, yet they all chose to fix their eyes on a mighty God whose understanding is far deeper and higher than ours and who promises to make a way when all paths seem to be closed.

If we look only at our circumstances, we will surely be disoriented and derailed by fear and discouragement. Instead we can follow the example of those heroes of our faith who looked to God for strength and peace in the midst of the storms. "Put your hope in the LORD both now and forevermore" (Psalm 131:3).

In the months before my (Kathy's) mother died, she was in and out of the hospital many times. My sister and I were utterly worn out from a year of watching her suffer. One particular night during a week when she was home—frail, weak, and exhausted from the fight—I settled her in bed and then sat down at the piano. The song that poured out of me included these lines:

I don't have to wish upon a star
I'll go on because of who You are

What else did I have but the hope that somehow God would make sense of it all? I yearned to hold on to Him and not to anger. I wanted to cling to Him and not to bitterness. Pushed to and fro by the storms at sea, I held tight to the strong buoy of my soul, determined to look not at the water but at Him.

I later had the privilege of sharing that song at my mother's funeral service. Amid my grief, I found a strange and sweet relief in knowing she was free and somewhere in the heavens, reunited with my father. With that knowledge and the assurance of the hope I have in God, I sang confidently and boldly those words I'd written just a few months earlier, "I'll go on because of who You are."

Keep On Keepin' On

Hope has a name. Hope never leaves. Because of these truths, we can hold on to Hope—but the decision to do so lies with us. When that alarm goes off in the morning, we must choose whether to greet the day with hope or with despair, to go on with God or just go on.

Here's what the writer of Hebrews had to say about persevering in hope no matter our circumstances:

> We'd better get on with it. Strip down, start running—and never quit! No extra spiritual fat, no parasitic sins. Keep your eyes on *Jesus,* who both began and finished this race we're in. Study how he did it. (12:1–2, MSG)

Study how He did it. If we want to hold on to an eternal, hope-filled perspective, we must look at how Jesus did it.

> Because he never lost sight of where he was headed—that exhilarating finish in and with God—he could put up with anything along the way: Cross, shame, whatever. (12:2, MSG)

Jesus never lost sight of the goal. That is the key to pressing onward with hope. He endured the cross and the shame heaped upon Him in order to free us from the weight of our sin and to give us hope for the days to come.

When you find yourselves flagging in your faith, go over that story again, item by item, that long litany of hostility he plowed through. *That* will shoot adrenaline into your souls! (12:3, MSG)

How can we grow weary and lose heart when we remember all that He has done for us and all He has promised to do in the future? Hebrews 10:23 says, "Let us hold unswervingly to the hope we profess." You know why? "For He who promised is faithful."

He is faithful. So hold tightly to His hand. Hold on to Hope.

Thoughts to *Noodle* On

1. Describe the last situation in which you found yourself thinking, like Elijah, *I've had enough, Lord.* How did you handle it?

2. What are some activities or people that drain your hope? some that feed it?

3. List at least three examples of God's past faithfulness that you can bring to mind whenever hope starts to slip away.

4. Write out your own psalm, pouring out to God all your hopes and concerns. Wrap up with a few of the things you know to be true about Him, things that give you hope in His faithfulness.

Abundant Love

One word
Frees us of all the weight and pain of life:
That word is love.

—SOPHOCLES

Chapter 7

God's Love for You

Discover a love that satisfies
your heart's deepest longings

D o you love music as much as we do?

I (Ellie) am quite a fan of all things Gershwin, Porter, Armstrong, and Fitzgerald. Who can resist tunes like "Someone to Watch over Me," "What a Wonderful World," or "Our Love Is Here to Stay"? Somehow they make me feel nostalgic for an era I know only through other people's stories, old movies, and sepia-toned photos.

Kathy was raised on big-band music. Her parents kept the radio tuned to an AM station that played lots of Frank Sinatra, and she describes how on Sunday mornings the crooning of Ol' Blue Eyes wafted through the house along with the fragrant aroma of the "gravy" her mom was stirring up for the family meal.

Of course we both cringe every time a radio deejay uses the word *oldie* to describe "All You Need Is Love" or one of our other favorite songs from the sixties and seventies. It seems like just yesterday we were first dancing to "Love, Love Me Do" by the Beatles or listening to James Taylor and Carly Simon vow that their commitment would last "till the sun dries up the sea." And who could forget John Denver's poignant request to "let me always be with you" in his beautiful declaration of eternal, undying love for his wife in "Annie's Song"?

Whatever your age or your particular taste in music, and whether you still use a turntable or download to your iPod, chances are that many of your favorite musicians have written and sung about love. But any musical stroll down Memory Lane eventually leads us to Reality Drive.

I don't like to be the bearer of bad news but…John left Annie, Carly left James, and Paul left Heather. People we count on *don't* always watch over us, love is *not* always here to stay, and the headlines remind us daily that it's *not* such a wonderful world.

No, I'm not a cynic, nor am I experiencing mood swings. (A hot flash now and then maybe.) You could call me a realistic romantic. I love the idea of love and happy endings as much as anyone. But I know that life doesn't always work out that way.

I am not mocking those incredibly talented musicians. I believe that when they expressed their love through song, they meant those words with all of their being. But here's the problem: human love is only…um…human. If there's one thing I've learned by age fifty, it's that people make lousy saviors. None of us have perfected the art of love, and even the most devoted lovers will occasionally let each other down. We are imperfect people, plagued with a tendency toward self-centeredness. Yet each of us was born with a longing to experience love in its full glory and perfection. It's what we were created for: relationship with the One who *is* love.

The Real Thing

In the previous chapters we've talked about faith and hope, the first two ingredients of truly healthy and holy living. We've also looked at some of the things that can distract us from feasting on abundant life and the ways we can make room for what really matters.

Now it's time to turn our attention to love, the third key ingredient God offers to satisfy our souls as we continue the process of becoming all that He created

Let's *Dish* About...
the Lover of Our Souls

KT: I love being in on conversations with married women when they're talking about what their husbands do for a living. I often interrupt and say, "My husband created heaven and earth. Pass the coffee." That always makes them pause for a moment! Seriously though, God has been a great husband, honoring me and covering me, never leaving me. What's your favorite image of God's love?

EL: I feel very comforted when I picture Jesus as the Good Shepherd. Although He is so much more than that, I rather like to imagine Him strolling with His rod and staff.

Shepherds are strong and firm, and yet they are patient when little lambs get out of line. They are fiercely protective, and they know each member of the flock intimately: birthmarks, battle scars, personalities, predispositions. The shepherd knows his sheep well, and he knows how far they can wander without stepping into dangerous territory.

A pastor once told me that the shepherd occasionally uses the crook of his staff to give a temporary limp to a lamb that wanders away. He will then carry the lamb for a week or so, and the small creature becomes accustomed to the smell, the voice, and the heartbeat of the shepherd. By the time the leg heals, the lamb has learned to rely on the shepherd. Knowing how safe and serene life is near the shepherd, the little one no longer desires to wander.

There are many artistic depictions of Jesus carrying a little lamb on His shoulders. I like to fancy myself as that little one and feel incredibly loved that He would choose to care for me—and to carry me when I find it difficult to move forward through the rocky paths of life.

us to be. "For right now," Paul writes, "until that completeness, we have three things to do to lead us toward that consummation: Trust steadily in God, hope unswervingly, love extravagantly. And the best of the three is love" (1 Corinthians 13:13, MSG).

Why is *love* the best? Because love is what prompted the most incredible gift we have ever been given. Out of the sheer greatness of His love, Jesus laid down His own life so that we could experience life to the full (see John 10:10–11). Without love—God's wonderful, unfailing, compassionate love—abundant living wouldn't even be a remote possibility because we'd have nothing in which to put our faith and no one from whom to draw hope.

> This is how God showed his love among us: He sent his one and only Son
> into the world that we might live through him. This is love: not that we
> loved God, but that he loved us and sent his Son as an atoning sacrifice
> for our sins. (1 John 4:9–10)

God loves us. That reality is the beginning of everything. *God loves us.* That reality changes everything. *God loves us.* That reality radically impacts the outcome of everything.

Everything God does is an expression of love, because love is God's nature. Make no mistake: His isn't the schmaltzy stuff of love songs and poems and greeting cards. God's love is the original, priceless, genuine article.

Let's look at just a few of the ways in which God's love is unlike any other.

God's Love Is Unmerited

In Romans we read, "At just the right time, when we were still powerless, Christ died for the ungodly. Very rarely will anyone die for a righteous man, though for a good man someone might possibly dare to die. But God demonstrates his own love for us in this: While we were still sinners, Christ died for us" (5:6–8).

Did you catch that? *When we were still powerless. While we were still sinners.*

Unlike those people in our lives whose attitude says, "Don't even talk to me until you get your act together," God loves us when we are unlovable and undeserving, and He pursues us until we stop running. (Both of us have been tackled on a few occasions.) As it says in Titus, "he saved us, not because of righteous things we had done, but because of his mercy" (3:5).

Mercy is such an incredible concept. After fifty years, I (Ellie) am still not fully able to grasp it. I am quite aware of how often I need mercy, and yet I have certainly not mastered giving it. If there is one portion of the population to which I generously extend mercy, I believe it would be my kids. This mother's heart has a huge soft spot that is quick to forgive seventy times seven. I am sure it's all connected with the placenta and that cord, but regardless of what Freud has to say, the ties between mother and child are strong, and mercy flows freely in my children's direction.

The first time I held those babies in my arms, I realized they were completely helpless and fully dependent on me for every need. And what did they have to do to win my affection, loyalty, and life savings? Not a thing. After just one glance at their tiny selves, I would have walked to China—backward, on glass, naked—for them. Okay, maybe the glass could be dirt. The point is, I was smitten, over the moon in love with those little Italians. Without hesitation, Frank and I would care for our little Lofaros and provide for all their needs and most of their wants. They would be the focus of our attention for decades to come. Frank was especially pleased to have a son, since Jordan is the only one in that family line to carry on the name. I will spare you the details of Frank's patriarchal decrees and his celebration of Jordan's one-day-old body part.

The love of a parent is the best illustration I can think of to describe God's love for us, and yet it still falls short. Yes, we bear God's image, much as bambinos bear a strong resemblance to their parents, but He loved us *before* we took His name as our own. In addition, if you'd known what a pill your child would be down the road, you might have had a few reservations about giving him your heart in those early moments of acquaintance. By contrast, God knew from long before the moment we entered this world exactly how twisted our hearts would be and how we'd break His own heart down the road, yet He has always loved us fully and without hesitation.

God's love is completely unmerited. It cannot be earned or deserved. It is based solely in His unfathomable mercy and grace.

God's Love Is Unconditional

Although Jesus's love compelled Him to die for us before we even knew He existed, we often behave as if we must work to retain that love once we've promised to follow Him. It's as if we have a mental to-do list of all the things it will take to earn and keep His approval: attend church and Bible study regularly, work in the church nursery, deliver meals to shut-ins, maintain a flawlessly cheerful disposition—and that's just for starters.

If we somehow fail or sin, if we fall short of the ideal Christian in any way, something in us seems to believe that we have to start all over. We have to work our way up to deserving the Lord's affection once again.

But God's love doesn't come with strings attached. Our behavior does not determine His love. We cannot do anything to convince God to love us more, and we cannot do anything that will make Him love us less. As Kathy likes to say, "You *can't* out-sin the love of God!" And Lord knows she's *very* glad about that. (Just camouflaging my own issues!)

When we repent of our sins—when we acknowledge what we have done wrong and ask for God's forgiveness—He promises to forgive our sins and then to throw them as far away from us as the east is from the west (see Psalm 103:12). We aren't geography experts, but that seems far enough to suggest He's not planning to retrieve our sins later so He can rub our faces in them.

You may wonder, *But doesn't He sometimes get disgusted with my selfishness? Doesn't He ever get tired of my whining and complaining? Won't He eventually get fed up with my failures and lack of faith?*

No. Never. It's just not in His character to stop loving you.

God's heart aches when we fail, not because He loves us less, but because He continues to love us so very deeply and because He wants us to experience abundant life. God is not mad at you. He is not disgusted. Though you may still be dealing with the consequences, He is not punishing you for what you did in 1989. He loves you completely, and He loves you perfectly.

You need only to read a few stories of people in the Bible to recognize that God is merciful, forgiving, and has a sense of humor about our frailties. If you don't think you are qualified to be or to do what He has called you to, then you are the perfect candidate for the job. And you're in good company, according to the Scriptures:

Moses stuttered.
David's armor didn't fit.
John Mark was rejected by Paul.
Timothy had ulcers.
Hosea's wife was a prostitute.
Amos's only training was in the school of fig-tree pruning.
Jacob was a liar.
David had an affair.

Why can't God use you?

Solomon was too rich.
Jesus was too poor.
Abraham was too old.
David was too young.
Peter was afraid of death.
Lazarus *was* dead.
John was self-righteous.
Naomi was a widow.
Paul and Moses were murderers.
Jonah ran from God.
Miriam was a gossip.
Gideon and Thomas both doubted.

Why can't God use you?

Jeremiah was a bullfrog! (Just making sure you're awake.)
Well, he *was* depressed and suicidal.
Elijah was burned out.
Samson had long hair.

Noah got drunk.

   John the Baptist was a loudmouth.

      Martha was a worrywart.

         Mary was lazy.

Why can't God use you?

Are your personal issues anywhere on that list? Could you be one who doesn't hear God's calling because you're convinced you've been disqualified from His love and from His service? I heard a preacher once say, "God doesn't call the qualified. He qualifies the called." When you protest, *Lord, I can't,* God says, *You can do all things through Me* (see Philippians 4:13).

God's Love Is Unselfish

One of the stereotypes about Italians is that we like to grant favors. At first, that sounds quite lovely and generous, but the downside is that some choose to view those favors as loans that they expect to be repaid upon demand. Surely Italians are not the only ethnic group with this problem. While you may be imagining dirty money and card games and loan sharks, I am thinking about the friend who drops off a meal when you're sick and then manages to work a mention of her generosity into every conversation. Or the relative who offers you a ride when your tire goes flat, then weeks later hits you up for gas money. Stereotypes can certainly ring true when it comes to particular individuals.

Sadly, many of us view God's gift of justice, in the sacrifice of His Son, Jesus, on our behalf as a two-part bargain rather than a true gift. We wait in dread of the day He'll call us—or worse, our children—to be missionaries in some mosquito-infested country. Or we suspect that He'll someday require us to sell all of our worldly goods and give the money to charity. Or maybe He'll insist that we give up whatever activity we find most pleasurable so we can demonstrate the depth of our commitment to Him by way of scrubbing toilets at the church. But God's gifts to us are not intended as bribery or extortion. He's not looking for what He can squeeze out of us.

God delights in you just because you're you, not because of anything you do for Him. Jesus gave His life for your sins, and He asks nothing in return. His is a pure love, truly unselfish in every aspect.

The Gift That Keeps On Giving

Jesus died not only to give you eternal life, free from the bondage of sin and death, but also to give you life worth living right here, right now. He longs to be in relationship with you, not for what He gets out of it but because He's so excited about what He can give to you.

Take a look at the familiar words below, quoted from 1 Corinthians 13:4–8:

Love is patient, love is kind. It does not envy, it does not boast, it is not proud. It is not rude, it is not self-seeking, it is not easily angered, it keeps no record of wrongs. Love does not delight in evil but rejoices with the truth. It always protects, always trusts, always hopes, always perseveres.

Love never fails.

Now read it again, substituting the name of Jesus Christ for the words *love* and *it*. If you try putting your name, your mate's name, your best friend's name, your mom's name, or your hero's name in there—it doesn't work! But when you insert Jesus's name for the words *love* and *it*, you can immediately see the beauty, consistency, and integrity of His heart toward you.

Unlike those who might flatter us with words like "I love you, so don't ever change," God's love is all about change. Yes, He loves you just as you are, but He knows that your life can be so much more—more joyful, more fulfilling, more peaceful, more purposeful, more satisfying on every level. And in His love He offers everything you need to experience that change. The psalmist and shepherd David wrote of God:

You will make known to me the path of life;
In Your presence is fullness of joy;
In Your right hand there are pleasures forever. (Psalm 16:11, NASB)

God delights in showing you where and how to walk so that you can experience the full richness and joy of life. He invites you into His presence so that He can give you the pleasures He designed especially for you. We're not talking about material wealth or physical gratification, although those may be part of His intended blessings for you. Primarily though, the pleasures God offers are those that come when you allow the presence of Jesus *in* you to shine *through* you.

God's love desires your deepest good. Rather than being a cheerleader watching from the sidelines, He wants to be intimately involved in your life. He offers to be your accountability partner, your faith-fitness trainer, your life coach. What He allows to happen in your life may not bring immediate joy, but it is always for your ultimate good. He never asks, *What have you done for Me lately?* but, *What have you allowed Me to do for you lately?*

> *Quannu amuri tuppulìa, 'un lu lassari 'nmezzu la via.*
> **When love knocks, be sure to answer.**

All for the Love of You

Most people are familiar with the words of John 3:16: "For God so loved the world that he gave his one and only Son, that whoever believes in him shall not perish but have eternal life." Is it possible that those words have become so familiar that we've lost sight of what they really signify? When we consider more closely what it means that God gave His Son out of love for the world, we gain a deeper understanding of just how unselfish this love is.

Isaiah 53 gives us a vivid, albeit disturbing, picture of the price Jesus paid for us to know both eternal life in heaven and abundant life on earth:

Surely he took up our infirmities
    and carried our sorrows,
yet we considered him stricken by God,
    smitten by him, and afflicted.
But he was pierced for our transgressions,
    he was crushed for our iniquities;
the punishment that brought us peace was upon him,
    and by his wounds we are healed....

He was oppressed and afflicted,
>   yet he did not open his mouth;
he was led like a lamb to the slaughter,
>   and as a sheep before her shearers is silent,
>   so he did not open his mouth....
He was assigned a grave with the wicked,
>   and with the rich in his death,
though he had done no violence,
>   nor was any deceit in his mouth....

He poured out his life unto death,
>   and was numbered with the transgressors.
For he bore the sin of many,
>   and made intercession for the transgressors. (verses 4–5, 7, 9, 12)

Jesus endured indescribable pain, all for the love of you. Without a doubt, He understands and cares about your deepest longings, concerns, and sorrows.

If you asked, *Jesus, do You know what it's like to be lonely?* He would answer, *Oh yes. I was so lonely in the Garden of Gethsemane. I felt abandoned and sad. My friends wouldn't sit with me or stay awake. They kept leaving and falling asleep.*

If you asked, *Jesus, do You know what it's like to be depressed?* He would answer, *Oh yes. That night in the garden I was so overwhelmed that I perspired blood from my forehead.*

If you asked, *Jesus, do You know what it's like to grow up in a single-parent home?* He would answer, *Oh yes. My mother was widowed at a young age. Whispers about the timing of my birth subjected her to scorn from some people in our community. She was sometimes concerned about providing for us.*

If you asked, *Jesus, do You know what it's like to be abused?* He would answer, *Oh yes. Mobs mocked Me and hurled things at Me. At one point My own family decided I was out of My mind.*

If you asked, *Jesus, do You know what it's like to be sexually molested?* He would answer, *Oh yes. I hung fully naked on that cross. The taunts were so hateful, and my outer dignity was stripped away.*

If you asked, *Jesus, do You know what it's like to suffer unthinkable agony?* He would answer, *Oh yes. As I hung on that cross, I tried to lift Myself in order to breathe, and each time, the nails tore deeper into My raw flesh.*

If you asked, *Jesus, do You know that it hurts to be human? Oh yes,* Jesus would say with a reassuring touch. *That is exactly why I came.*

Jesus endured all this and more because He desires to give you a life rich with fulfillment and meaning, even in the midst of difficult days. He wants to bless you in your coming and in your going. He loves you with an everlasting, unselfish love. Have you known that love? Jesus gently knocks, but He will not force His way in. He awaits your invitation.

God's Love Is Unfathomable

There is nothing quite like experiencing the love of God! It is the greatest gift we have ever been given. Here's what the apostle Paul wrote about it:

> I pray that you, being rooted and established in love, may have power, together with all the saints, to grasp how wide and long and high and deep is the love of Christ, and to know this love that surpasses knowledge—that you may be filled to the measure of all the fullness of God. (Ephesians 3:17–19)

God's love surpasses knowledge; it's beyond our understanding; it defies description. Yet something within compels us to share this amazing truth with others, even when we cannot find quite the right words.

Our friend Barbara Johnson, a popular speaker with the Women of Faith conferences, knew a great deal about the love of God. This dear woman, an eternal optimist known to many as the Queen of Encouragement, was deeply admired by all who had the privilege of meeting her before she went home to Jesus in the summer of 2007.

Having buried two sons and a husband, Barbara was well acquainted with heartache and grief. Yet she chose to focus her vision on God's goodness and Jesus's victory over the grave. She wrote and spoke to millions about her precious "deposits in heaven" and would say of each, "He's not gone. He's just gone ahead."

In November 2000, Kathy was invited to be the guest artist on Women of Faith's Caribbean cruise. She was told she could bring a friend for free. When she asked, I (Ellie) just knew (without even praying) that God would want me to sacrifice my time to this vital ministry opportunity. Needless to say, it was a wonderful week. Cruising is great, and free cruising is even better.

One evening Barbara stopped by our table during dessert. She placed one hand on my shoulder, the other on Kathy's, and said, "I would like a little time with the two of you." Given my own shame issues (more on this later), I immediately wondered what we did to get in trouble. But then she smiled warmly and asked, "Would you please come up to my room later?"

An hour later we knocked on her door, our minds filled with an excited sense of anticipation. Why did Barbara Johnson—this incredible, godly woman—want to talk with *us*? The cabin door opened, and there she stood, looking as if she had stepped off a movie set from the fifties. High-heeled pearl-toned slippers with fuzzy fur across the top peeped out from under her flowing silky purple robe. Her hair was brushed out, and for a minute I thought I was with Harriet Nelson or Donna Reed. She said, "Hello, girls. Come on in!"

The three of us sat on the couch in her dimly lit, handsome stateroom, which had a double-wide balcony with wall-to-wall glass doors. She proceeded with apparent forethought. "You know, we old-timers are like eighteen-wheelers. We've been on the road for many, many years, and we've covered a lot of miles. Some of us will be coming off the road soon. We expect you younger ones to carry the load and keep moving." It seemed a holy and prophetic moment, and we listened quietly as Barbara spoke of her growing desire to see her two sons who had preceded her to heaven.

Then she suddenly stood up with a broad smile, and in a much lighter tone announced, "I have a surprise for you girls out on the balcony!" We stepped outside, and she delightedly said, "Well, here's your surprise. I give you the moon!"

A gorgeous full moon hung in a velvety sky scattered with brilliant stars. We could hear the rhythm of the breaking waves as the ship cut effortlessly through the pitch-black Caribbean Sea. The whitecaps produced by the sharp bow were mesmerizing.

A set of high-powered binoculars rested on the table of the balcony, and we took turns looking through them. The three of us—Donna Reed between Laverne and Shirley—leaned against the railing to take in that incredible view, breathing sighs of wonder and awe. Then Barbara began to recite these words from memory:

The love of God is greater far than tongue or pen can ever tell;
It goes beyond the highest star and reaches to the lowest hell.
The guilty pair, bowed down with care, God gave His Son to win;
His erring child He reconciled and pardoned from his sin.

Oh, love of God, how rich and pure! How measureless and strong!
It shall forevermore endure—the saints' and angels' song.

Could we with ink the ocean fill and were the skies of parchment made,
Were every stalk on earth a quill and every man a scribe by trade;
To write the love of God above would drain the ocean dry;
Nor could the scroll contain the whole, though stretched from sky to sky.[1]

Zia Aida's Zeppoli

Share these bite-size bits of heaven, and remember to thank God for the gift of taste buds!

Ingredients

- 2 packets instant yeast
- 1/2 cup warm water
- 3 tablespoons butter, melted
- 3 egg yolks
- 3 cups all-purpose flour
- 1/2 cup sugar
- 1 teaspoon salt
- 1 to 1 1/2 cups milk
- vegetable oil, for frying
- powdered sugar
- ground cinnamon (optional)

Wow. Imagine the hairs on the back of my neck standing up when she softly uttered that last verse down toward the deep water and up toward the massive sky. I shall never forget that breathtaking scene in the theater of life.

Just three months later, Barbara was diagnosed with a brain tumor, which she lived with for six more years. She may not have known the details of her future on that moonlit night, but she knew the promises of her God and felt both comforted by and confident in His love. She fully enjoyed His presence and provisions for her life.

Not having been raised in the church, I was unfamiliar with the words Barbara quoted on the cruise ship that night, but I found out almost a year later that they were the lyrics of the beloved hymn "The Love of God" by Frederick Lehman. How beautifully and poignantly his words celebrate the unfathomable love of our God.

Cooking Instructions

1. In a medium bowl, whisk yeast and water together. Add butter and egg yolks. Whisk well. Add flour, sugar, and salt. Whisk again. Add milk, a little at a time, until mixture resembles a thick batter.

2. Cover bowl with plastic wrap, and allow dough to rest at room temperature for 1 hour.

3. Preheat oil to 360 degrees. Using a tablespoon, drop batter into hot oil. Fry until golden brown, about 3 to 4 minutes, turning if needed. Remove and drain on paper towels.

4. Place fried sweet dough balls in a paper bag; add powdered sugar and cinnamon, if desired. Shake the bag; serve warm.

Delizioso!

God's Love Is Unending

As finite humans, we will never fully comprehend the infinite love of God. We can't fully understand it or explain it, but if we are believers, then we have surely experienced it and are promised that we can never be separated from it:

> Neither death nor life, neither angels nor demons, neither the present nor
> the future, nor any powers, neither height nor depth, nor anything else in
> all creation, will be able to separate us from the love of God that is in
> Christ Jesus our Lord. (Romans 8:38–39)

Nothing, absolutely nothing, can put an end to God's love. In Jeremiah 31:3 He declares, "I have loved you with an everlasting love." If your heart belongs to God, if you've chosen to lean on Him in faith, you can count on His loving-kindness "to infinity and beyond!"

> From everlasting to everlasting
>   the LORD's love is with those who fear him,
>   and his righteousness with their children's children—
> with those who keep his covenant
>   and remember to obey his precepts. (Psalm 103:17–18)

God's love outlasts our failures and frailties. It outlives cancer and chemotherapy. It endures through our temper tantrums and pity parties. And if we allow it to do so, God's love will carry us through everyday annoyances and unexpected trials.

In the third chapter of Lamentations we read, "Because of the LORD's great love we are not consumed, for his compassions never fail. They are new every morning; great is your faithfulness" (verses 22–23).

Don't you love that? Today really is a new day, cleansed from all the mistakes of the past and shining with this glorious truth: God loves you. He loves you. *He loves you!*

Maybe we don't need to toss out those old love songs after all. You do indeed have *Someone* to watch over you. *Godly* love is all you need. With *Jesus,* it is a wonderful world. *He* can fill up your senses, and *He'll* always be with you.

Thoughts to Noodle On

1. Think for a moment about your favorite love song. What about it specifically speaks to the longings of your heart?

2. The Bible is jam-packed with verses about the love of God. Which one is your favorite to rely on when you need to know you matter to Somebody?

3. What in your life, if anything, prompts you to wonder if God could really love you? How does Romans 8:38–39 help answer that for you?

4. How would you answer if Jesus asked, *What have you allowed Me to do for you lately?* In what way(s) is His love a special comfort to you today?

Chapter 8

Loving God

When pleasing Him is your highest goal, everything else falls into place

One breezy summer afternoon I (Kathy) took a drive with my friend Val to Leipers Fork, a quaint little town not too far from my home in Nashville. The two of us enjoyed taking in the sunlit views of trees and farmhouses along the way. It was one of those rare Saturdays when I was not on the road and so was free to do whatever I wanted. I felt like a kid let out of school early.

Among the many shops we browsed through that day was an elegantly decorated candle boutique, filled with all kinds of fascinating little things. I knew immediately that I would not be leaving empty-handed. Both of us began sniffing through this garden of wax. Somehow, cards and candles have the same effect when you are with a friend. A giggle followed by, "Read this." Or an, "Ooohhhh... smell this one." Each new discovery is way too good to keep to yourself; it needs to be shared.

Amid this olfactory feast, I smelled something familiar. The musky scent, a bit like patchouli, was similar to what I call a Catholic smell that often permeates the air at masses, confessions, and funerals. I have often bought patchouli-scented candles because their aroma is so connected to memories of my childhood. This candle-store fragrance had the same effect; with every whiff, I was transported back to my visits to see Mother Cabrini.

Every year my mom took my sister and me to the Saint Frances Cabrini Shrine in New York. There, within a crystal altar, lies the preserved body of the first naturalized American citizen to be named a saint. We would kneel and pray, get a Mother Cabrini souvenir, then leave.

As you might have guessed, the whole experience spooked me. The first time I walked into that chapel, I didn't know if she would rise from the dead, or maybe she would just lie there and wink at me. But Mother Cabrini, resting there in her nun garb, looked exactly the same every year: waxy and dead. The waxy effect, I realize now, was because her head is somewhere in Rome, so what I was seeing was a wax representation. No wonder those visits left such an impression on me!

Of course, I have learned since then that she was a powerful yet humble servant of God whose work as a nun made a difference in the lives of many. During those childhood visits, I simply understood that she was holy, even though I'm quite sure I had no clue what that meant. In light of all the fuss made about her, I concluded that she must have been a friend of God. Someone special indeed.

As I stood in that little store in Leipers Fork, breathing in the memories along with the fragrance, I whispered a prayer: "Somehow, Lord, continue to make me a woman after Your heart. I want to love You better. I would love to be remembered as Your friend."

Put Your Heart in It

The idea of being a friend of almighty God may seem a little presumptuous, and yet we know that God called Abraham "friend" (James 2:23), and He spoke to Moses "as a man speaks with his friend" (Exodus 33:11). Jesus was known as "a friend of tax collectors and 'sinners'" (Luke 7:34). What's to stop us from being His friends as well?

As we read in the previous chapter, God loves each of us, without limit and without condition. Nothing we can do will make Him stop loving us or convince Him to love us more.

So what response does such love prompt within us? How are we to handle this gift? What will we do about the abundant, abiding love that God so freely offers to each of us? Stuart Briscoe suggests that we must first recognize God's love, then respond to God's love, and finally, reflect God's love. In the simplest terms: we see it, accept it, and share it. Sounds terrific—where do we start? We love Him in return, and we share His love with others. "We love because He first loved us" (1 John 4:19).

When we think about what God wants from us, so often a list of rules and regulations comes to mind: keep the Ten Commandments; tithe at least 10 percent; attend church every time the doors are open; give generously to missions; don't cheat or drink or smoke or chew, and don't hang out with those who do. And that's just for starters. Some of us could provide a list of don'ts stretched longer than the line of cars on the Brooklyn Bridge at rush hour.

In this regard we sometimes resemble the Pharisees and the Sadducees, the two major religious groups in Israel at the time of Christ. They were all about keeping the Law, and they argued continually about which sets of rules were most crucial to righteousness: the 613 laws identified by the Pharisees or the shorter list drawn from the Pentateuch and interpreted by the Sadducees. Both sets of religious leaders condemned others for failing to meet their rigid standards, standards they themselves could not possibly live up to.

These two groups disliked and distrusted each other, but they were allies in trying to trip Jesus up by drawing Him into their debates about which rules led to true holiness. One day a Pharisee, an expert in the Law, posed this question: "Teacher, which is the greatest commandment in the Law?"

Jesus's answer rocked their world: "'Love the Lord your God with all your heart and with all your soul and with all your mind.' This is the first and greatest commandment" (Matthew 22:36–38).

This is remarkable. It is huge! Our love is a big deal to God. Out of all the rules and regulations that have been held up as the guiding principles for life, the greatest is to "love the Lord your God with all your heart and with all your soul and with all your mind."

All of us performance-oriented overachievers need to stop for a moment or two and think about this. What's the most important thing we can do for God? Love Him. Period.

Oh, How I Love Jesus

The concept of loving God feels vague and beyond comprehension to most people. We love our mothers, we love our husbands, we love our kids, we love our friends, we love our mothers-in-law—well, some of us do. A married friend with a difficult mother-in-law once told me (Kathy) that the definition of mixed emotions is watch-

Let's *Dish* About...
Ditching Our To-Do Lists

KT: Ellie, as you strive to love God with all your heart, mind, and soul, what impact does that have on your daily to-do list?

EL: For me it means following the old formula for J-O-Y: it has to be Jesus, others, yourself, in that order. I'm always weighing my day's schedule against what—or who—it is I'm supposed to be yielded to. Yes, I have a lot to do, but I must be willing to flex. Sometimes that means putting my agenda on hold so I can be kind and listen to a neighbor, a friend, or a kid who just needs to be heard.

It seems to me a dangerous idea has crept into our culture, a subtle message that we women will find our greatest fulfillment in meeting our own needs and focusing primarily on our own little worlds. Yes, we absolutely need to care for our families and make time for ourselves, but we need to have a larger view—a God's-eye view—of what matters. Otherwise we're missing out on countless opportunities to interact, to be in community with others and help meet their needs. At the end of the day,

ing your mother-in-law drive off a cliff in your new Mercedes. I *think* she was joking. Anyway, we love our dogs, we love our neighborhoods, we love our freedom, we love good pizza. Although Ellie lives in Virginia and I live in Nashville, both of us return at least twice a year to Mecca (New York) to indulge in the real deal! I love so many things. I love the ocean, I love great music, I love interior design, and I love the stars at night. Couldn't we each fill a book with the dozens of things we love?

we need to have a sense that it wasn't just about our lists but about tending to the needs God has placed in our paths moment by moment.

KT: For me, if I don't take opportunities throughout the day to acknowledge the big picture, to remember there are eternal things going on, I soon find that hours fly by and I haven't even talked to God. Then I wonder why I have anxiousness in my gut and my mind is racing as I get into bed.

Being aware of God as I go through my days—talking to Him in the immediacy of any situation—puts it all in perspective. Then I can view everything through an eternal filter, and I see more clearly and feel greater peace. On the days where it's all about the tasks, I feel as if I bumper-car my way through life, knocking into things everywhere I turn. When I deliberately keep that eternal perspective through the course of the day, it's not like the days are easy, but I definitely notice a smoother flow, as if I'm on track with God.

EL: We all need to remember that very few items on our to-do lists will have lasting value. Though mundane and unexciting duties are a necessary part of life, the time we spend with God and caring for the people He created is never wasted.

But using the word *love* when it comes to how we feel about God is completely different. I did not understand loving God until I was twenty. If you had asked me in my younger days whether I was a Christian, I would have said, "Yes. I'm Italian. What else would I be?" I know now that there was no substance behind my answer. Yes, I went to church, albeit not consistently. We celebrated Christmas and Easter with ten-course feasts that concluded with dessert, then started over again in an hour. At every Easter dinner Grandpa Esposito would dip a stick of palm he kept from Palm Sunday into a jar of holy water. Then as he sat at the head of the table, we would be doused with "the blessing" as if he were the pope. Of course I was a Christian. *Not!*

Like many other people, I had simply adopted the faith of my ancestors without making a personal choice or commitment. I was a small-*c* Christian—whether by birth or inference or default—but my faith was certainly not my own. By contrast, Ellie teaches that a capital-*C* Christian is someone who wakes up in the morning and says, "I am Yours, Jesus. I am reporting for duty. What plans do You have for me today?" A capital-*C* Christian is someone who would absolutely give his or her life for the cause of Christ.

> *Dimmi con chi vai chi ti diro chi sei.*
> Tell me who you go with,
> and I'll tell you who you are.

In 1978, I came to a point of personal realization that I had religion but not a relationship with God. I had never before really looked at the life of Christ for myself. As in many Italian homes, crucifixes hung in different rooms in our house, so on certain days when the cross caught my eye, I would give Him a quick thought. But I did not know what an intimate God He was. I had no idea that He yearned for me to know Him, that He truly loved me, that He was real. It was such a glorious revelation when I finally "got it"—when the religious veil fell off my eyes and I realized that I could have a personal relationship with this God I had "believed in" from afar. It changed my world. I became a capital-*C* Christian. I was in love. I began writing about Him and singing about Him in the musical style I'd been using in the clubs. My family was baffled as my weekends shifted from engagements at a local hotel or bar to performing at an area church or coffeehouse.

My newfound faith left my family wondering if I had joined a cult. My uncles informed me that my father was rolling over in his grave and that I was killing my mother. It was the most moving, exciting time of my life, and yet I was making my mother so worried and sad. She didn't understand. Praise God, over time she eventually saw God's hand on me. It was undeniable. My mother had completely given her life to Jesus by the time she left this earth.

To Know Him Is to Love Him

As our own experiences show, religion does not bring about a love affair with God. Relationship does.

To know Him, personally and intimately, is to love Him. That's why we've chosen as the theme verse for our Spaghetti for the Soul conferences Psalm 34:8: "Taste and see that the LORD is good." Not, "Come close and see." *Taste.* Not even, "Taste and see *if* you like Him." It says, "Taste and see *that* the LORD is good." How will you know if you don't taste?

If a friend bit into an apple and asked you how it tasted, you would look at that person like she was crazy. How could you possibly know whether it was bitter, sweet, ripe, or rotten unless you tasted it for yourself? When people go on about their opinions of Jesus or who they think He is, do you ever wonder if they have truly tasted of Him? Do they know that He is good?

I (Kathy) have found that a common misconception among women is that Jesus somehow wants them to go back to the way life was before women had the right to vote. They're convinced He'll cramp their style. It makes me so frustrated because I know the liberation Jesus brings to a woman's soul. He invites us to discover true love and genuine self-respect. He offers promises and plans to change a woman, not to chain a woman. He gives wisdom based on an eternal perspective so we can make decisions that protect us from the misery that springs from needy temporal choices. Those who have tasted of God's goodness know that He doesn't pull us backward but instead beckons us forward into something better.

The late-nineteenth-century British theologian Dr. Alfred Momerie preached poignantly and powerfully about loving Jesus:

> If you do not love Him, it must be because you do not know Him. Either He is seldom in your thoughts, or you think of Him as a dogma rather than a person.... Remember how wonderfully, like no one before or since, He combined all conceivable excellences. He had the tenderness of the most womanly woman, and at the same time the strength of the manliest man.... He was keenly alive to the paramount importance of the Spirit and eternity; and yet no one was ever so thoughtfully considerate for men's temporal and bodily welfare—He ministered to them in their bereavements and their diseases, He was not unmindful of their hunger and thirst.... He avoided no effort, He shirked no sacrifice, He shrank from no anguish by which He might serve the race in revealing God and reconciling man.[1]

There are so many reasons to love God, if only we will open our senses to experience all that He offers and all that He is.

Father of the Bride

A dear pastor friend of mine (Kathy's) works with Life Outreach International on behalf of the poor and needy in India. I've had the privilege of joining Dwayne Weehunt in his efforts a couple of times, and I have really enjoyed being with him and his family. He is so ministry minded—a big bear of a man with an equally big heart.

I will never forget sobbing on the streets of Mumbai, completely undone by the sight of dozens of little boys homeless and in such need of love. I could hardly catch my breath as I wrestled with my anger at the desperate circumstances of those children and worked through my own questions of what God allows in this broken world. Dwayne provided the gentleness I needed, and I felt as if Jesus was right there with me, brokenhearted at the state of mankind and the world.

Later that day I was reminded of an Emily Dickinson quote:

> I shall know why, when time is over,
> And I have ceased to wonder why;

Christ will explain each separate anguish
In the fair schoolroom of the sky.[2]

On my second trip to India, we spent one day filming women and children bathing themselves and washing their pots in dirty, diseased water out in the rural parts of the country. It was "wonderfully" grueling, and I knew this footage would prompt hearts to give so that the quality of those precious lives could improve.

We were all sweaty and dirty and tired as we drove back to the hotel, everyone eager to take a long hot shower. Dwayne and I sat in the backseat, talking about life and all sorts of things. He said he had been praying for me since the last time we were together because something I said had stayed with him. The comment was one I'd made many times before about relating to God more as my husband than as my Father. Of course, I know that He is both, but I more easily see myself as the bride of Christ than as the daughter of the King.

No one had ever really made much of it before, but as we sat in that van together, Dwayne gently challenged me about my perspective. He said that as a father, it broke his heart and that he had been praying for me in that specific area during the previous year. He yearned for me to truly know the Father heart of God.

As he spoke, a lump formed in my throat. When certain places in your heart are poked at a little, you tend to either come out swinging or let the Holy Spirit bring the balm you need to heal. I knew I needed to hear Dwayne's words. As I listened, I was able to share my deep lack and bankruptcy in that area. My dad was kind, and as far as I could tell, he was a good man. But he was taken from this earth so soon that I missed out on much of what a father brings to a daughter. He worked long hours, so I didn't really know him.

I then listened with a touch of envy as this earthly father described his heart leaping at the sight of his children. He adores them, protects them, and prays for them. As Dwayne tried to open my eyes to what I was missing by not welcoming God into the role of my heavenly Father, he told stories of his love for his children. One story in particular will stay with me for the rest of my life.

His now-teenage daughters were six, four, and two when they decided to fix him a special Father's Day breakfast. From the kitchen came clanging, clinking, and some noises that suggested things breaking. Still Dwayne and his wife decided to stay in bed, honoring the girls' request to not leave the room.

When the children finally carried in his breakfast on a tray, Dwayne said, the pancakes were raw and everything was just as awful as you might imagine such a meal would be. When he later went into the kitchen, it looked like a war zone. "But you know what, Kathy?" he continued. "It delighted my heart. They were trying to please me."

I was so touched to have this illustration to help me receive more of the love that the Father heart of God yearns to give me. My willingness to find out what pleases Him and what delights His heart is much more important to Him than any mess I may make along the way. It will all be cleaned up by His grace.

Cousin Connie's Chicken Cutlets

A fool-proof recipe for the hungry, the finicky, and those who are "out the door" right after dinner.

Ingredients

- 2 pounds boneless, skinless chicken breasts or tenders (or turkey breast)
- 1/4 cup olive oil
- 3 eggs, beaten
- 1 to 1 1/2 cups dry Italian-flavored bread crumbs

Additional ingredients for Chicken Parmesano:

- 1 1/2 cups prepared marinara sauce
- 6 to 8 slices of mozzarella or provolone cheese
- 3/4 cup grated parmesan cheese

Cooking Instructions

1. Rinse and dry breast pieces, and trim off all fat and tendons. (Slice meat into strips or nugget size, if you prefer.)

Delighting Daddy

When we truly love people, we yearn to be near them. We want to bless them, give to them, serve them, and care for them. That is why Paul tells us to live as children of light and "find out what pleases the Lord" (Ephesians 5:10).

One hallmark of Jesus's life on earth was His total reliance on His heavenly Father. Their relationship revealed a mutual love that defined every word, action, and choice He made. Jesus said of the Father, "I seek not to please myself but him who sent me" (John 5:30). His example provides fresh inspiration as we look for

2. Season meat with salt and pepper. Dredge each piece in beaten eggs, and then coat with bread crumbs, assuring each piece is evenly coated. Pat well with fingers or fork, turn over, and repeat.

3. Generously coat the bottom of a skillet with oil, then heat on medium-high. Cook chicken in hot oil until no longer pink inside, 3 to 5 minutes per side. Cut a piece open to check doneness. If crumbs are browning quickly while meat is still uncooked, lower heat; do not let it burn. Place on a platter, dabbing excess oil with paper towel.

4. Serve hot or warm. Great for sandwiches and snacks the next few days.

Variation: For Chicken Parmesano, spoon prepared sauce on cooked chicken breasts, place sliced or shredded cheese on top, and place under a broiler for 2 minutes. Sprinkle grated parmesan cheese on top.

Serves 6.

ways to love God with all our hearts, souls, and minds. How can we please God? By staying as close to Him as possible. Jesus gives us a beautiful word picture in John 15:5: "I am the vine; you are the branches. If a man remains in me and I in him, he will bear much fruit; apart from me you can do nothing." To remain in Jesus means to find your identity in Him, to let His character define you and direct your actions.

I (Kathy) have noticed at different seasons in my life how deeply my outlook and behavior are affected when I let go of God's hand. Sometimes I haven't been "eating" regularly of His words in the Scriptures. Maybe I am not communicating with Him consistently. Whenever or however I start living apart from Him, I begin to see how quickly my ways change. I lose His perspective. I become more anxious. I gossip more. I quickly become agitated with people. I operate through my own strength and not His.

By contrast, when we stay connected with Him, our lives will bear much fruit, in the form of love, joy, peace, patience, and all the other things that delight God.

Is it your goal to please your heavenly Father? If so, then your love for Him will color every moment of your day. When your son forgets his math homework or your husband comes home from work long after supper is cold, your goal is to please God rather than to straighten out the offenders—although you probably wouldn't mind if the Holy Spirit laid a little conviction on them. When your employer announces a series of layoffs, your goal is to please God by responding with grace and peace. When the doctor says, "We need to biopsy that lump," your goal is to please God by trusting Him rather than letting panic take over.

As a capital-C Christian, your desire is to be a peacemaker rather than a troublemaker, an encourager rather than a discourager, a giver rather than a taker. Your days are shaped by sincerely asking what Jesus would do—and then doing it!

"What's Next, Papa?"

When we first fall in love with Jesus, we feel such a thrill and enthusiasm, as in any relationship that is new. But some of us start to lose our eagerness even as we grow in knowledge of God. Our hearts fail to keep pace with our heads. We may live in the church world, but we have lost our intimacy with and tenderness for Jesus.

Work for God must be motivated by a love for God, or it becomes nothing more than hypocrisy, something which the heart of God opposes. Consider His words to the church of Ephesus in Revelation 2:3–5:

You have persevered and have endured hardships for my name, and have not grown weary.

Yet I hold this against you: You have forsaken your first love. Remember the height from which you have fallen! Repent and do the things you did at first.

Jesus knows how our zeal tends to wane when the difficulties of life overwhelm us. That is why He speaks so frankly and honestly, warning that we will follow Him in His sufferings: "If anyone would come after me, he must deny himself and take up his cross daily and follow me" (Luke 9:23). Sure, we would all love a cozy, carefree life, but this isn't heaven, and lack of suffering is not the way of the gospel.

We read in 1 Peter 4:12–13, "Dear friends, do not be surprised at the painful trial you are suffering, as though something strange were happening to you. But rejoice that you participate in the sufferings of Christ, so that you may be overjoyed when his glory is revealed."

The difficulties of life should not surprise us; instead, they should bring us joy—joy that comes from participating in the sufferings of the One we love. From the very first days of the church, loving Jesus has involved personal sacrifice, laying down our own lives, and taking up the cross of His suffering. One early historian who witnessed the heroism of the Christians in the early church as they were about to be slaughtered by the lions wrote, "The day of their victory dawned, and they walked from prison to the amphitheater as if they were walking to Heaven, happy and serene in countenance."[3]

Can we, too, face the challenges of life with gladness rather than fear? *Absolutely*, when we're filled with love and trust for our heavenly Father. In Romans the apostle Paul wrote:

This resurrection life you received from God is not a timid, grave-tending life. It's adventurously expectant, greeting God with a childlike "What's next, Papa?" God's Spirit touches our spirits and confirms who we really are. We know who he is, and we know who we are: Father and children. And we know we are going to get what's coming to us—an unbelievable inheritance! We go through exactly what Christ goes through. (8:15–17, MSG)

As the NIV translates verse 17, "We share in his sufferings in order that we may also share in his glory." Our love for God gives us confidence to face whatever life throws our way, as we say with childlike expectation and trust, "What's next, Papa?" We know that, whatever it may be, He won't ask us to carry the burden alone. Instead, He gently offers this invitation:

Come to me, all you who are weary and burdened, and I will give you rest. Take my yoke upon you and learn from me, for I am gentle and humble in heart, and you will find rest for your souls. (Matthew 11:28–29)

Whether our troubles result from living in a fallen world or arise directly from our own sin, we sometimes believe that things are in such a mess that God can't possibly still be sticking around. We bring Him down to our level, convinced He doesn't want anything to do with our junk. But in truth, your Father God is delighted when you turn to Him for help, even if you've made the mess yourself. Not only that, but He comes alongside to offer His strength to help you carry the load of life. Do you love Him enough to trust Him with your mess?

Psalm 147:11 says, "The LORD delights in those who fear him, who put their hope in his unfailing love." God loves us with a supernatural, unconditional, everlasting love, and He delights in receiving love from us in return. We show that love by putting our trust and hope in Him no matter what's happening in our lives.

Lavish Gifts of Love

Even as we strive to walk though this life with an eternal mind-set, knowing the glory that will one day be ours because we've endured suffering with Christ, we can find joy in knowing there is also great reward in following Jesus here on earth. First Corinthians 2:9 says, "No eye has seen, no ear has heard, no mind has conceived what God has prepared for those who love him."

When you love God, the sky's the limit! There is great reward in the here and now as well as the hereafter. God's love compels Him to give to us. And He does it so lavishly. He not only gave His beloved Son to the world, but to each of us He offers deliverance, peace, power, joy—and the list goes on. We can wake up every day, like children on Christmas morning, in excited expectation of what He has prepared for us! Heaven is the ultimate gift after you've opened up all the others throughout your lifetime. The evangelist John R. Rice once imagined:

> I went to Heaven and the Angel Gabriel and I were walking down the street. I said, "Hey, Gabe, what is that beautiful building over there?"
> "John, I feel bad about that."
> "What is it?"
> "Well, I don't think you will want to talk about it."
> "Why? I want to see it."
> So Gabriel takes me over...to a beautiful building with fine glass and marble—the prettiest thing! Everywhere there are tables and cupboards and cabinets with packages wrapped in beautiful paper with ribbons and with greetings. I ask, "What in the world are all these things?"
> Gabriel says, "These are things we had wrapped up for people but they never did call for them."[4]

God has amazing things planned. We can't even imagine what He has in store for our lives—but He won't force any of it on us. We will experience His good and perfect gifts only when we stop making demands about what *we* want out of life and instead simply give ourselves over to loving Him at every opportunity.

All I Want for Christmas

I (Kathy) remember challenging myself about the depth of my Christianity and my love for God one particular Christmas season. Life is always hectic, but it gets even crazier when the beginning of December rolls around. Everything feels just a little more intense. In addition to the physical flurry of my work schedule and holiday activities, memories of the past and concerns about family, relationships, and the future seem to whirl around me like Dorothy's dream outside her window when the tornado hit. I often found myself careening on an emotional roller coaster at that time of year, and I yearned to have peace through it all. I wanted to truly celebrate the season.

I was reading from The Message one cold December morning when I came to

Ephesians 1:11–12: "It's in Christ that we find out who we are and what we are living for. Long before we first heard of Christ and got our hopes up, he had his eye on us, had designs on us for glorious living, part of the overall purpose he is working out in everything and everyone."

Who are you, and what are you living for? Those are challenging questions. But the answer is right there, in Christ: God has "designs on us for glorious living."

But we won't experience glorious living until we give God room to work His masterful design in our lives. I bristle at the phrase "Take it or leave it—this is just the way I am." I intentionally stopped it from coming out of my own mouth years ago. What a cop-out, especially for a Christian. You might as well just say that you refuse to change. The goal of every believer should be to become more like Jesus, to follow His example of surrender to the Father.

So that winter morning, I asked God to fill me and change me. I knew that my desire to love Him more was a gift from Him. I renewed my complete surrender to Him that day, wholeheartedly giving Him access to my life and my heart.

In the days that followed, as part of my commitment to be more deliberate about focusing on the truth and what matters, I posted on the refrigerator door a running list of spiritual, physical, and emotional reminders:

- *What am I living for?*
- *What occupies my heart?*
- *What worries me and consumes me?*
- *What is on my plate right now?*
- *What shouldn't be on my plate?*
- *How do people perceive me?*
- *Am I hiding?*
- *Do I truly love God?*

When I take that kind of inventory, it helps me to be authentic before God and people. I long to be the real deal. I long for the Lord to have a great reputation in me, and I don't want to sit around making excuses for myself.

No one ever said that the journey to holiness would be a joyride, that's for sure. So I must keep asking myself those hard questions. Do I really want to live for Him? Do I really want to be obedient? Do I really want to become like Him, or would I prefer to just mix a little of God with a lot of myself? You know, kind-of-sort-of be a Christian—on my terms.

No, I want the deeper journey: a life infused with love for God, the kind of love that says, *Do with me what You will.* When I meet genuine Christians—when I see Jesus in their persons—I want to weep. There is such peace in their eyes. They exude a kindness and a graciousness that is warm and inviting. In the presence of such people I feel as if I am sitting under a tree of wisdom, finding rest as I listen and learn. It's beautiful. It's supernatural. It's an invitation to a higher life, to more abundant everything. That's what I want—for Christmas and for always.

Oh, come let us adore Him! Let us love Him with our lives and our speech. Let us love Him with our actions and in our relationships. Let us build lives in which God's presence can dwell. May everything we are and everything we do declare our love for Him.

Thoughts to *Noodle* On

1. As you consider the idea of friendship with God, what words would you use to describe such a relationship?

2. What are some of the things you *do* to show your love for God? How does your perspective on your to-do list change as you consider the greatest commandment, as identified by Jesus?

3. Do you find it easier to relate to God as your Father or to Jesus as your Bridegroom? Explain your answer.

4. List five things you love about God, based on your own experience of tasting and seeing His goodness.

Chapter 9

Loving Others

The recipe for a richer life includes giving yours away

Our friendship was born in December 1990 in the women's wing of a Long Island psychiatric hospital. No, we weren't patients! I (Ellie) was there with a group of women from my church to share some Yuletide cheer with the residents. In the middle of "Silent Night," Kathy walked in the side door of the community room. The group began to stumble and slur and finally stopped, leaving us abruptly in "Silent Afternoon." They were, in a word, star-struck. *A real, live, famous vocalist is in our midst!* I was, in a word, nonplussed. *Ignore her! She's a mere mortal! Keep singing!*

Years later we laughed about how determined I was not to be impressed or to behave like a fan. Truth be told, I *was* impressed with how kind and humble she was that day as she sang along with us, served cookies, poured punch, and hugged every patient. I liked her.

In the days that followed, the two of us started to get to know each other. I'll let Kathy take the story from here...

Two months after I (Kathy) first met Ellie, my mom was diagnosed with terminal cancer. I remember sitting in the waiting area of Sloan-Kettering Hospital in New York City, feeling as alone as I have ever felt in my life. I looked out the window at a dreary, cold rainy day that seemed to cloak the city in the same despair that smothered my heart. Then around the corner of the hospital lobby came Ellie, wearing a rain-soaked coat and wringing out her umbrella. God had impressed on her heart to come see me. So she left two babies home with her sweet husband, Frank, and drove over an hour to be with me at the hospital. It was then that I knew I had a friend for life.

What drew the two of us together initially was seeing the other person offer the love of God to others in tangible ways. Truly, love for others is one of the most attractive features of any person we know.

Let the Love Flow

In chapter 8, we looked at Jesus's earth-shattering statement to the Pharisees: " 'Love the Lord your God with all your heart and with all your soul and with all your mind.' This is the first and greatest commandment." Right on the heels of this declaration come six important words: "And the second is like it."

And what is the second most important commandment? "Love your neighbor as yourself" (Matthew 22:37–39).

Loving others is right up there with the greatest commandment of all! *Why?* Because loving others is a vital aspect of loving God. It's all tied together.

As disciples of Jesus seeking to please our heavenly Father, we are to follow His example of unselfish, sacrificial love. In John 13:34–35, Jesus gave His followers a direct command: "Love one another. As I have loved you, so you must love one another. By this all men will know that you are my disciples, if you love one another." *Love one another.* It's not a suggestion; it's a commandment.

If love is the hallmark of those who follow Jesus, why does God bother to make it a commandment? Won't it just happen naturally? Sadly, no. Becoming a person characterized by love is part of the ongoing, lifelong process of growing more like Christ. Although we have the Holy Spirit's help in the process, it's up to us to decide to follow His lead in love.

Most of us would find it easy to be great Christians—saints, really—if it weren't for other people. They're always getting in the way, with their neediness and their pettiness and their failure to consistently do things our way. Have you ever noticed the similarity between controlling women and God? They both love you and have a plan for your life. We laugh, and yet isn't that why we so often fail at expressing true love? We attach all kinds of strings and conditions, using our love as leverage rather than simply giving it freely, the way God does.

So Jesus highlighted the second great commandment because true love—unconditional, unmerited, unshakable love—won't flow through us unless we first receive it from God. It's a supernatural phenomenon. And even then we have to make a deliberate, conscious choice to let the Holy Spirit love others through us.

First Peter 1:22 says, "Have sincere love for [others], love one another deeply, from the heart." Yet so many things get in the way of being able to live that way. We lead busy lives, and we feel as if we don't have time to deal with other people's issues. We have Bible studies to attend, conferences or retreats to organize, and meals to prepare for the church potluck. Who has time for people?

To complicate things further, we were born with a sin nature. The channels through which love should flow tend to get clogged with pride, stubbornness, bitterness, and unforgiveness. With all the junk we hold inside of us, it's a wonder that the pure love of God finds any place to seep in.

But when we let the Holy Spirit clear out the rubbish and fill us to overflowing with God's love, that love will spill out of us and onto everyone around us, including close friends and family members as well as the strangers we encounter through the course of a day. You can splash the love of God onto other people only when the river of life is flowing inside of *you.*

> *Ama il prossimo tuo come te stesso.*
> ## Love thy neighbor as thyself.

The First Epistle of John mentions *love* forty-three times in its brief 135 verses. John tells us about a great God and His limitless love—a love that heals us, renews us, and makes us whole. "Dear friends," writes John, "since God so loved us, we also ought to love one another. No one has ever seen God; but if we love one another, God lives in us and his love is made complete in us" (4:11–12).

As we consistently follow the example of Jesus and allow God's love to be made complete in us, our relationships will reflect a love that is genuine, humble, forgiving, selfless, and enduring.

Get Real

Few would argue that we live in a world largely devoid of love. Why does this vital ingredient, for which our hearts were made, seem glaringly absent from the world

Let's *Dish* About...
Practical Ways to Show Love

EL: Kathy, can you think of a time someone showed you love in a tangible, no-strings-attached kind of way?

KT: About fifteen years ago I was struggling financially. I'd been out of the music business for a while, first to take care of my dying mom and then grieving her death. When I returned to work, I felt like I would never get back on my feet. One night as I was preparing to give a concert, a couple approached me. They said that my music had blessed them for years and they wanted to give me something back. Their gift was a substantial amount of money. I was floored. It was like manna from heaven. God's love and concern for us never ceases to amaze me.

EL: I find it incredible how God works through people to touch us with His love just when we most need some encouragement.

news, from our neighborhoods, from so many marriages, and from our increasingly isolated lives? Is it because people confuse attraction and emotion with love and then find their hearts crushed when those counterfeits can't stand up to the pressures of life? Our deluded culture has been taken in by pure love's imposters, which make people feel good in fleeting, crumb-sized increments.

It stands to reason that if people don't know the God who is the Author of love, they can never know true love. What comes to mind is the old ad slogan that admonishes us to "Accept no substitutes." We benefit in so many ways when we

You know, in Gary Chapman's book *The Five Love Languages,* he helps people identify the way they prefer that others show love to them. He suggests that we choose words of affirmation, quality time, gifts, acts of service, or physical touch. Well excuuuuse me for being a hog, but I like receiving *all* of those expressions of love! On my thirty-fifth birthday, my creative husband managed to deliver all five at once. I was home with a six-month-old, a toddler, and a preschooler. Forget the Wonder Years; those were the Wet Years. I was overweight, underpaid (my salary was approximately zip), and losing my battle to stay ahead of the laundry and the meals.

Frank wrote me a beautiful letter thanking me for the three miracles. He also gave me a certificate for a massage and a voucher to spend four hours with a tech guy at a local video place to edit all our baby videos. He officially reinstated date night and took me out to a romantic dinner that evening. There, he presented me with an airline ticket to Rome, where I would spend a memorable week with my aunt Ida.

Now *that's* love! I think I'll keep him.

take that instruction to heart in how we receive and express our love for God, self, and others.

People all around us are hungry for the real thing, but they have sensitive hypocrisy radars. They recognize phoniness, and they are watching us, looking not for perfect but for real.

Romans 12:9–10 says, "Let love be without hypocrisy.... Be devoted to one another in brotherly love; give preference to one another in honor" (NASB). The church should be the safest place to belong, a refuge in which you can honestly share all that you are, your struggles, and some of your deepest thoughts. Yet true freedom often eludes us because we're too busy trying to hide our shame and our stuff. Where we are wrestling with doubt, what we are doing, what causes us fear or trouble, what addictions may be strangling us as we keep a smile pasted on our faces—all these remain untold. For the little some of us reveal, we may as well be sitting in the dark with our mouths taped shut and our hands tied behind our backs. But we cannot experience the life-giving power of God's grace unless we confess those areas in which we most need His resurrection power.

Just as Jesus used the death of Lazarus to reveal the glory of God, so removing the stone that seals our lives in darkness allows His light and power to shine forth. But remember what Mary, the sister of Lazarus, said when Jesus asked for the stone to be removed from the tomb's entrance? *But, Lord, he'll stink.*

How many times does the fear of how others will respond to our stench—or of our discomfort with the idea of another person's odoriferous junk—keep us from being exposed? But God wants our spiritual sisters and brothers to unwrap our grave clothes, and He calls us to do the same for them. If only all of us could trust that when we come out of our caves of secrets and deadness and sin, we'll be welcomed into the arms of our loved ones, even if we stink.

For people who are not acquainted with God personally, their perception of Him stems from what they see in those who profess to follow Him. Oh, to live life consistently, not afraid to show the cracks, not ever putting on masks to hide the hurts we carry around. God does not ask us to be perfect. He asks that we let Him reach others through us as we live our lives authentically. In doing so, we give hope to all those who wonder if God is who He says He is: a God whose love is strong enough to handle even our darkest realities.

Let Grace Pour Down

In Ephesians 4:2 Paul encouraged us to "be completely humble and gentle; be patient, bearing with one another in love." That sounds good, doesn't it? And yet how difficult it can be to live up to those words. Why is that?

We all want mercy, but somehow we have a hard time passing it forward. None of us like to be on the receiving end of judgmental comments, and yet we're all guilty of making them from time to time. It's like that kids' show on Nickelodeon where they poured green guck all over everybody: we "slime" one another with disapproval and disdain rather than recognizing our mutual need for God's cleansing touch.

In His last evening with the disciples before He went to the cross, Jesus carried out an incredible act of humility. He washed their feet, using His own hands to scrub away the grime and grit accumulated during a day of walking on dusty roads. When He had finished this task—something usually reserved for a lowly servant—He said, "I have set you an example that you should do as I have done for you. I tell you the truth, no servant is greater than his master, nor is a messenger greater than the one who sent him" (John 13:15–16).

Who are we to judge another as unworthy of our love or too grubby for grace when Jesus gave His very life out of compassion for that person?

I (Kathy) find myself blown away by the reality that God provides an endless shower of grace under which anyone can find cleansing and refreshment for her soul. Part of me wants Him to let people sweat it out a little. Let them ponder the rain not coming. How black-hearted I can be. But when I think of my own heart and what I am capable of, I hear myself pleading, *Pour! Let it pour!*

I can't help but think of Paul's statement: "Christ Jesus came into the world to save sinners—of whom I am the worst. But for that very reason I was shown mercy so that in me, the worst of sinners, Christ Jesus might display his unlimited patience as an example for those who would believe on him and receive eternal life" (1 Timothy 1:15–16). I thank God for His unlimited patience with me even as I repent of my impatience with others.

As much as I have wanted to be a great lover of God and people, I've failed in countless ways. For so many years I was just like Pigpen, walking around just spreading my dust and grime. Thank God, He's blown much of it off, but remembering the past reminds me how desperately I need the grace of God—and how I need to extend it to others.

Yes, I have done my share of dishing out the green stuff, but lately I find myself asking God to change my heart posture so that I look at others with this attitude: *I have the log and you have the speck.* In other words, in humility I want to give others the benefit of the doubt, realizing I don't fully know their pain, their backgrounds, or their problems. I continue to press my defenses down so that I don't get in the way of God's defending me. When someone hurts me deeply, I can choose either to shower quickly under the cleansing of God's words or spend weeks picking and plucking crusty, moldy, prickly feelings of resentment.

How easily we are offended, and what a difference it makes when we choose instead to listen and humble ourselves, being people of few words so that we can hear when God truly wants us to speak. Rather than judging people when I disagree with their words or actions, I want to extend mercy and grace. Doing so means I desperately need God's heart and mind in dealing with others, in offering compassion rather than taking offense.

Throw Away Your List

As Italians, we sometimes feel more at home with grudges than with grace. The very word *vendetta* comes straight from our ancestors. But maybe that's a human thing rather than a cultural thing. We often love out of brokenness rather than wholeness. We are easily offended. We nurse our wounded pride. We cling to bitterness.

This is completely contrary to the way Jesus interacted with people. He was never defensive. He wasn't irritable. Jesus wasn't moody or touchy, and He didn't keep a record of wrongs. Jesus didn't boast, and He certainly didn't celebrate when people failed. Jesus never said, "Well, he got his!" As a matter of fact, He went so far as to say, "Love your enemies and pray for those who persecute you" (Matthew 5:44).

It is just like Jesus to speak those words and act that way and to ask us to do what He does. He calls us to walk the way of the gospel—and the way of the gospel is like no other. *Love our enemies?* That goes against our every human, let alone Italian, instinct. And that's precisely the point: what is natural to God is unnatural to us, and so we must lean on His supernatural strength.

We cannot fully know what is happening in the spiritual realm when we pray for our enemies, or how God is working in their hearts. But in truth, much of the time the Lord wants to get to the heart of us. Our prayers and our willingness to forgive and to love ultimately change *us*.

It doesn't really matter how the other person responds, because we're called to

Boobala's Basil Pesto

Whip up a double batch and deliver a warm baguette, fresh pesto, and a caring smile to a neighbor.

Ingredients

- 2 cups packed fresh basil leaves
- 1/4 cup *pignoli* (pinenut) or walnut pieces
- 1/4 cup grated Parmigiano Reggiano
- 3 tablespoons extra-virgin olive oil
- 2 tablespoons water
- 1 large clove garlic
- 1/2 teaspoon salt
- 1/2 teaspoon freshly ground pepper

Cooking Instructions

Place all ingredients in a food processor; pulse a few times, then process until fairly smooth or to the desired consistency, scraping down the sides occasionally.

Pesto can be heated and served on pasta, chicken, or fish; served cool on crackers; or oven baked on focaccia bread, pizza dough, thinly sliced French bread, or pita.

give love that is unconditional and unmerited. You don't love others because they are perfect. You love them in spite of their imperfections.

As we saw earlier, Jesus said, "Greater love has no one than this, that he lay down his life for his friends" (John 15:13). Most days we can't lay down our pride, let alone our lives! We tend to keep a running tally of offenses. Some of our Italian family members aren't particularly shy about discussing their personal lists:

- "They didn't give, so I'm not giving."
- "Don't seat her by me at the wedding!"
- "He never paid me back!"
- "She never said that she was sorry. I'm certainly not apologizing."
- "She's not allowed to come to the funeral!"
- "He never calls, so I'm not about to phone him."
- "Don't you remember what she said to me last Christmas? I'll never forgive her."

Many of us have lists a lifetime long—longer if we're carrying our family's register of wrongs. We can either continue adding to the lists we've been handed, or we can cut them up in the shredder of God's love and forgiveness.

In 1 Peter 3:8–9 we're told, "Live in harmony with one another; be sympathetic, love as brothers, be compassionate and humble. Do not repay evil with evil or insult with insult, but with blessing, because to this you were called so that you may inherit a blessing." Only by tossing out our lists and grabbing hold of forgiveness can we experience the full blessing of a life rich with love and healthy relationships.

Lose Your Life; Find Your Way

One of the most difficult aspects of following Jesus is letting go of those things we think are important and allowing Him to replace them with what truly matters. Laying down our lives doesn't necessarily mean physical death, although that's certainly a possibility for many believers around the world. More often, however, the cost of carrying the cross involves the death of our self-centeredness. Romans 8:13 warns, "If you live according to the sinful nature, you will die; but if by the Spirit you put to death the misdeeds of the body, you will live." Becoming more like Jesus, allowing God to have His way with us, means a deliberate putting to death of the things that hinder us, so that we can have truly abundant life and give it to others.

Jesus said, "Unless a kernel of wheat falls to the ground and dies, it remains only a single seed. But if it dies, it produces many seeds" (John 12:24). In other words, when we choose love—of God and of others—over self-interest, God turns our lives into fertile fields where His purposes can thrive. "If you grasp and cling to life on your terms, you'll lose it, but if you let that life go, you'll get life on God's terms" (Luke 17:33, MSG).

Our prayer to Him each day should be, *Lord, how can I join You in what You are doing?* Consider these verses:

Even the Son of Man did not come to be served, but to serve. (Mark 10:45)

This is how we know what love is: Jesus Christ laid down his life for us. And we ought to lay down our lives for our brothers. If anyone has material possessions and sees his brother in need but has no pity on him, how can the love of God be in him? Dear children, let us not love with words or tongue but with actions and in truth. (1 John 3:16–18)

Be imitators of God, therefore, as dearly loved children and live a life of love, just as Christ loved us and gave himself up for us as a fragrant offering and sacrifice to God. (Ephesians 5:1–2)

Give, and It Will Be Given to You

We have no idea how much richer and more fulfilling our lives can be when we carry the love of God to others through service and sacrifice, especially when it takes us out of our comfort zones.

Earlier I (Kathy) wrote of my experiences traveling to India with Life Outreach International. I never would have imagined that my life's journey would lead me to minister in the slums of Mumbai, but there I was with a film crew to document the dreadful conditions in which hundreds of thousands of children live every day. Our goal was to raise money for an orphanage and provide some of those children with homes and guardians.

I went to India in hopes of showing God's love to others, but I encountered Jesus there in ways I never expected. I had read that Mother Teresa often spoke of seeing Jesus in the eyes of the impoverished. I thought I knew what she was talking about—knowing that the breath of God is in every person. But I quickly learned that she was referring to so much more.

Little ten-year-old Israel had never been to a day of school in his life. This kind and funny and beautiful child had always lived on the street. We purchased a sweater for him from a street vendor. A short time later, I began to weep from a heart heavy with grief over the devastating conditions in which those little ones live. Israel and the other children wanted to know why I was crying. The interpreter explained that I was crying for them, God's children. Israel turned to me, raised his sweater sleeve to wipe my eyes, and said, "Thank you." How quickly a gift from God had been used in return. I was humbled beyond words.

Later that same day, a member of our ministry team purchased tea and cookies for some of the boys. I was sitting in the car, trying to compose myself, when a hand tapped at the window. A boy offered me one of the two cookies he had been given. When I declined his generous offering, he pleaded with me. Remembering the Scripture story of the widow and her two small coins, I obliged so I wouldn't hurt his feelings. The boys then huddled together on a corner and split the other cookie among them. My heart both leaped and broke to be the recipient of such a lavish gift.

The next morning I visited a seven-year-old boy named Santush, whom we had discovered was very ill. Both of his parents had died within the previous year, and he was living with his grandmother in a space the size of a bathroom. Looking incredibly undernourished and dripping with perspiration from a fever, he greeted me with a weak smile and an outstretched hand as he sat on a bed of filthy rags. As I held his feeble body on my lap, we talked through the interpreter for a bit, and I then described his situation for the camera.

After a while, he glanced upward and said softly, "Pa-pa." I turned around to see a picture of his father on a shelf up above. I took it down and placed it beside us, then continued talking to the camera on his behalf. As I spoke, his tiny hands tenderly stroked the image of his father's face, over and over again. All the while, dust and dirt from the picture kept falling on my pant leg. Then this sick and grieving child gently reached down and brushed it off. I could hardly catch my breath. I literally felt the hand of Jesus. It was one of the most beautiful feelings that I have ever had run through my body.

All I thought about the rest of the day was Jesus saying, "Whatever you did for one of the least of these brothers of mine, you did for me" (Matthew 25:40). How little we understand about the truth of His words, yet how readily He reveals it to us when we reach out in love.

As I tried to love others in the name of Jesus, He met me again and again in the eyes, the smiles, and the hands of those abandoned children of India who offered their "riches" freely to this orphaned Italian girl.

Make Me a Blessing

Helping the less fortunate is high on God's list of priorities for those who love Him. "He who is kind to the poor lends to the LORD, and he will reward him for what he has done" (Proverbs 19:17). This goes beyond sending in a check or dropping money in the offering plate. Yes, your contribution to foreign missions, your sponsorship of a needy child, or your participation in serving a Thanksgiving dinner to the homeless all make a difference. But what about the smaller daily things you can do for others? Have you taken a second look at your blessings to see how God wants you to use them for His purposes?

God's not interested in how big your house is but in how you use that house to bless people. God doesn't care about what kind of car you drive but about whether you use that car to offer someone a ride to the doctor or to help a senior citizen get out to the grocery store. God's not interested in your awards and diplomas but in how you invest your gifts and talents in the lives of others, without concern for what you'll get in return.

The life and teachings of Mother Teresa continue to inspire us long after her death. Though she may have suffered with doubt, she never allowed it to derail her acts of love and service to "the least of these." In her book *A Simple Path,* she quoted an excerpt from the Litany of Humility, which originated with Rafael Cardinal Merry del Val and became the daily prayer for the Missionaries of Charity order founded by Mother Teresa. This prayer so eloquently expresses the principle of losing our lives so that we may find the abundant life God offers:

Deliver me, O Jesus,
From the desire of being loved,
From the desire of being extolled,
From the desire of being honored,
From the desire of being praised,
From the desire of being preferred,
From the desire of being consulted,
From the desire of being approved,
From the desire of being popular,
From the fear of being humiliated,
From the fear of being despised,
From the fear of suffering rebukes,
From the fear of being calumniated,
From the fear of being forgotten,
From the fear of being wronged,
From the fear of being ridiculed,
From the fear of being suspected.

Are you willing to lose your life so that you can love people God's way? Rest assured that when people cannot pay you back, God will. When you don't receive public credit, God makes a note in your record. When you serve quietly, without applause and out of the spotlight, God makes sure that you will receive the applause of heaven, as Max Lucado describes it.

We can't speak for you, but the two of us want to be soft and pliable and always ready for God to form His nature in us. That's the only way He can turn our hearts in new directions, freeing us to live with our thoughts centered on His desires rather than our own. Loving others is not easy, but it's what we yearn and pray for.

Legacy of Love

We believe that one of the key reasons God leaves us on this earth is so that our lives and our love will draw others to Him. Jesus said, "I chose you and appointed you to go and bear fruit—fruit that will last" (John 15:16). The fruit He produces in us will be irresistible to those who are hungry for the truth that satisfies, and as they see God's love at work in us, people will be drawn to taste and see for themselves that God is good.

We have to remember, though, that we don't produce sweet fruit on our own. This is why Jesus cautions, "No branch can bear fruit by itself; it must remain in the vine. Neither can you bear fruit unless you remain in me" (John 15:4). When I (Ellie) don't spend time soaking in God's Word, I catch myself acting like that talking apple tree in *The Wizard of Oz*. A hungry person comes along, desperate for some soul food. Instead of feeding her out of the riches God has given me, I slap her hand or start throwing things at her. Not literally, of course, but you wouldn't describe my attitude at those times as loving.

By contrast, when I find my delight in God, as Psalm 1 says, I become like a tree with roots that reach straight into a source of fresh water. I yield tasty fruit, and my leaves won't wither, no matter what the weather. This passage reminds me of the redwoods in California. Did you know that those towering trees actually have rather shallow root systems? Their strength comes from growing close together with other redwood trees and intermingling their roots. In addition, I learned from a forest ranger that root length corresponds to tree height. The farther the roots reach for nourishment, the taller the tree grows.

In much the same way, we remain spiritually strong and healthy by spreading our roots into the soil of God's Word, intertwining our hearts with His, and establishing relationships that offer mutual support and nourishment.

When I lived in New York, I was connected with an amazing group of women I called the "no problem" sisters. These were the church ladies who walked alongside me from the first days after I came to know Jesus, on through college, marriage, and my early days of parenting. I knew I could always count on them. If I needed help with the kids, I could call one of them. "No problem," they'd say. "We'll take care of it." Feeling under the weather and not up to cooking? "No problem." They were there with a meal. Need my house cleaned? "No problem." (Actually, I never tried that last one, but I'm sure they would have come through.)

Anyway, those women are who I aspire to be like when it comes to loving others. I want to be the cool lady on the block that all the teens feel safe sharing their problems with. I want to be the friend who can be trusted not to repeat your secret.

I want to be someone my family can depend on to love them through whatever comes along.

I believe that as we strive to be "no problem" sisters to the people in our lives, we're building a legacy of love that will last for all eternity. Have you given thought to how you will be remembered for the ways you have loved? Your ability to leave such a legacy is not limited by your circumstances, skills, or wealth; you are a daughter of the King, and you have complete access to His vast treasury of resources.

The extent of our potential impact was recently brought home to me (Kathy) by one of my nieces. I was having one of those weeks where I felt a little sad, a little lonely, and a little invisible. Even as I reminded myself that God really does love me and that I am not alone in the world, the questions lingered in my heart: *Do I really matter? Does my life make a difference?*

Resisting the impulse to crawl back in bed and stay under the covers, I made myself a cup of coffee and turned on my computer to check my e-mails. Scrolling down through my inbox, I saw one from my twenty-three-year-old niece Maria. The subject line simply said, "legacy." I began to read...

so God has been speaking to me a lot about legacy lately. and i know that is the direction he is taking women's ministries in minn. it's all about mentoring, grabbing hold of our rich heritage and running forward with it. allowing the legacy of those before us to live on, while leaving new legacy through pouring into and mentoring others. it made me think of how i want daughters so i can pass their mother's legacy down to them. then i thought how awful if i never got married or had daughters. who would i pass my legacy onto? then i thought of you. i thought how you have one of the greatest legacys i know of to pass down to a daughter. i felt sad for a second. but then i remembered...not only the thousands of women you have passed pieces of your legacy onto, but me. i am your legacy. everything I know about life and the way i want to live it i have learned from you. when people ask me how i came to be the way i am, live the passion and the romance i so desperately try, i say it was from watching you. my greatest mentor, my pal, friend and aunt—i love you. so, just wanted to say, thank you for the tremendous legacy!

love, your legacy, ri

What a gift—one of the most precious I have ever received. I could hardly catch my breath. I was held captive by the thought that Jesus had read my mind and knew my heart. I squeezed my eyelids together and then read it again. I smiled as I noticed that Maria writes on the computer the same way I do: all lowercase letters. I thanked God that my life matters to Him—how I live it, how I give it, how I love others.

What a privilege we have been given to be able to spend our lives giving God's love away. We ought to continually thank the Lord for the joy of letting His love shine through our lives, and we ought to reflect His goodness to people near and far. We truly can make a mark on eternity.

The apostle Paul says to "go after a life of love as if your life depended on it—because it does" (1 Corinthians 14:1, MSG). Only by truly loving others can we experience the full richness of abundant living.

That certainly is what Jesus did, and that's what the two of us want to do. How about you?

Thoughts to *Noodle* On

1. What are some of the things that get in the way of your loving others?

2. Describe a time when you felt judged by someone. Now think of a time when you judged another person. What different emotions did you experience in each situation?

3. Make a brief list of your material blessings, along with some ways God might be calling you to use them to help others.

4. What legacy would you like to leave behind? What steps can you take to start putting your plan into action?

Chapter 10

Loving Yourself

True contentment comes in learning to see yourself as God sees you

I (Ellie) was raised in the kind of household where you did not air the family laundry, under any circumstances. So when I started attending Kathy's concerts, I grew a bit uneasy listening to her freely and openly share her pain, her sins, and her pitfalls. Where I come from, you never tell those sorts of things, especially not to strangers. That stuff was meant to remain private.

Yet as I continued to watch, it became clear to me that Kathy's deliberate openness resulted in healing, growth, and humility for her, as well as a supernatural ability to touch people in very deep places. I've seen women line up out the door and down the hallway just for the chance to speak with her. Without a doubt, her transparency and utter desperation for the Lord help free others to experience repentance, surrender, and healing. She loves to say, "God is using the very places where I have scars to bring life and hope to others."

Well, isn't *that* special? Personally, I'm not all that eager to expose my flaws to others, no matter how much good it will do them or me. A good counselor would most likely say I have "shame issues." I don't know for sure since I have never sought professional help—a huge mistake, according to my kids. My husband, Frank, also thinks I should get help immediately. He swears I have ADD. He has assured me that with the proper treatment I will be able to focus, complete all my tasks, and lose weight as a bonus. What a sensitive guy.

Dino Bellini's Pasta e Fagioli

This used to be called "peasant soup." It is inexpensive, satisfying, nutritious, and delicious. Enjoy it with a crusty loaf, which in certain regions is called "peasant bread." You'll feel *rich*.

Ingredients

- 3 tablespoons extra-virgin olive oil
- 3 to 4 cloves garlic
- 3 basil leaves
- 3 cups water
- 2 tablespoons tomato purée, or 3 to 4 medium plum tomatoes
- 1 (15-ounce) can cannellini beans, rinsed and drained.
- 8 ounces orecchiette (or other small pasta)
- 1/2 teaspoon salt
- ground pepper to taste
- 1/4 cup freshly grated parmesan or Pecorino romano cheese

Cooking Instructions

1. Put a large pot of water on to boil for cooking the pasta.

Now where was I? Oh yes. Back to my shame issues.

I was raised in a happy, healthy, hearty family with more blessings than most. At the same time, our household was culturally patriarchal, socially competitive, politically conservative, spiritually nebulous, conversationally stifled, highly intolerant, and emotionally fractured. (I was a stutterer by the age of five). And you

---

2. In a large skillet, pour olive oil to coat bottom over low heat. Add garlic and cook, stirring, until fragrant but not colored, about 1 minute. Add basil and 3 cups water—bring to boil.

If you use tomato purée:

3. Add cannellini beans and 2 large spoonfuls tomato purée. Lower heat and cook approximately 20 minutes.
4. Meanwhile, cook pasta in the large pot of water, then drain. Add to skillet, along with salt, pepper, and grated cheese to taste.

If you use plum tomatoes:

3. Add tomatoes and seasoning; cover and increase heat to medium. Stirring occasionally, cook until tomatoes start to break down and release their juices, 5 to 10 minutes. Add beans, reduce heat to low, and simmer, covered, until heated through.
4. Meanwhile, cook pasta in the large pot of water. Then reserving 1/2 cup of boiled water, drain pasta and place in skillet. Add reserved 1/2 cup cooking liquid; toss to coat. The dish should be slightly soupy. Add salt, pepper, and grated cheese to taste.

Serves 4 to 6.

want to know why I have shame issues? This stuff is *exactly* why God arrived on the scene—and oh boy, am I glad He came!

Because of Jesus, I am not just your average overwhelmed, performance-driven, anxiety-riddled woman. According to Ephesians 1, I have been blessed, chosen, adopted, redeemed, forgiven, lavished with grace, and much, much more.

The same is true for you, if you have chosen to accept the gifts He offers to those who follow Christ. And yet so often we lose sight of this truth, blinded either by our pride or our self-contempt.

> *Zoccu è datu da Diu nun pò mancari.*
> **What is given by God can't be lacking.**

Although a healthy love of self isn't one of the two great commandments, Jesus's words—"Love your neighbor as yourself"—clearly indicate an assumption about how we view ourselves. You'll notice He never urged us to "loathe your neighbor as yourself" nor to "laud your neighbor as yourself." But as with so many aspects of the Christian life, loving ourselves in a healthy and balanced way is easier said than done. Manipulative messages from without and negative self-talk from within invade our thoughts and distort our perspective.

So let's take a look at what it means to love ourselves the way God intended and how doing so can bring contentment to our hearts.

Pride and Prejudice

I (Ellie) became a committed Christian at the young age of fifteen. I asked Jesus to come into my heart, fill me with His Spirit, forgive my trespasses, and be my constant companion. It is by far the best decision I have made in the last half century.

Though I have had my share of bumps, bruises, and trials, for the most part my life has been crisis free. I have been given a wonderful, godly husband, three healthy and (usually) terrific kids, financial security, and the privilege of sharing my gift of teaching with women in my own hometown on Wednesday mornings and across the country on weekends. My ducks are arranged in a reasonably neat row—or at least it looks that way from the outside.

Because God has led me down fairly smooth paths, I occasionally am tempted to lean toward a spirit of "religiosity." Sometimes I wonder why she can't get it together, or why he can't stop smoking, or why they don't work harder to pay their bills, or why that church is losing people every week. I am not proud of this tendency to bolster myself by looking down on others, but still I occasionally find myself repenting of my attitude of superiority.

Yes, I have done much good out of a desire to please an audience of One. But I've found it's also possible to do good things without pure intentions. Have you ever spoken more kindly than usual to a spouse or child in front of others? I have. Have you ever put money in the offering basket or tip jar because you knew a certain someone was watching? I have. Have you ever extended yourself to a person who was physically or mentally challenged with the thought of being admired by onlookers? I have. Have you ever given special attention to the famous or rich over the one with nothing to offer? I have. Sadly, our human nature expects to be noticed, applauded, thanked, and admired when we do something noble.

So often we look shiny and put together on the outside, but the closets of our hearts are crammed to overflowing with all the junk we don't want anyone to see. Jesus warned against such hypocrisy. In the twenty-third chapter of the gospel of Matthew, He verbally rebuked the religious leaders of the day who were more engaged in self-aggrandizement than self-assessment:

> Woe to you, teachers of the law and Pharisees, you hypocrites! You shut the
> kingdom of heaven in men's faces. You yourselves do not enter, nor will you
> let those enter who are trying to. (verse 13)

Jesus did not mince words. He railed against those who thought too highly of themselves. He had no fear of being deemed politically incorrect or socially harsh. In fact, Matthew 23 records seven "woe to you" warnings for those who have it all together in their outward appearance but whose hearts are not aligned with God's heart. Here's another one:

> Woe to you, teachers of the law and Pharisees, you hypocrites! You are like
> whitewashed tombs, which look beautiful on the outside but on the inside
> are full of dead men's bones and everything unclean. In the same way, on

the outside you appear to people as righteous but on the inside you are full of hypocrisy and wickedness. (verses 27–28)

God will judge those who elevate themselves, who cling to their self-righteousness rather than throwing themselves on the mercy that comes through Christ. Consider Saul of Tarsus, a savvy Jew whose blue-blooded lineage traced back to the tribe of Benjamin. He was born into a fine family, educated in the best schools, and trained by the most revered rabbis. He studied to be a lawyer and was accepted to the holy order of the Pharisees. What mother could want more for her son?

When he played a key role in squelching the Christian fanatics and became a main persecutor of the early church, Saul was literally and figuratively thrown off his high horse onto the Damascus Road. The fall (demotion) and accompanying blindness resulted in surrender (promotion) and "new eyes" for the apostle, who would go on to pen much of the New Testament. Paul got a fresh start—a do over, if you will—but he paid a high price. He went from being a revered and feared scholar and statesman to being a humble preacher who endured beatings, shipwrecks, imprisonment, deprivation, rejection, ridicule, and eventual martyrdom. Even the Christians refused to trust him for a long while.

Whether it involves a grain of corn, a mustard seed, or a newborn baby, a bit of dying always takes place in order to produce new life. (I have C-section scars to prove it!) That's why Paul later wrote, "I have been crucified with Christ and I no longer live, but Christ lives in me" (Galatians 2:20). The greater our pride, the more "self" God has to prune away to help us flourish spiritually.

Most of us are keenly aware of the great value God places on meekness and humility, but in our humanness, we tend to resist the instruction to "humble yourselves before the Lord, and he will lift you up" (James 4:10). We've bought into the idea that loving ourselves means always looking out for number one, and as a result, our culture, including the church in many cases, is experiencing an epidemic of self-centered, rude behavior. Yet, has this attitude brought any of us lasting satisfaction?

In one of the first Sunday school classes I (Ellie) ever attended as a teenager, the teacher shared the secret to full and lasting joy (which I mentioned earlier): put Jesus first, others second, and yourself third. In doing so, you spell J-O-Y. Kind of switched around from the culture's prescription, isn't it? That's because the ways of Christianity are often directly opposed to the ways of the world. Jesus upset the status quo two thousand years ago with His radical teachings, and we still have trouble wrapping our minds around them today:

- You must lose yourself to find yourself.
- Those who boast will be brought down.
- Humble yourself, and God will lift you up.
- When they slap your cheek, turn to them the other.
- When they take your shirt, offer your coat.
- When they demand you walk a mile with them, go two instead.
- The last will be first, and the first will be last.

You won't find that kind of thinking in *Self, Vogue,* or *Cosmo*! Instead the ads and articles shout, *It's all about you... You deserve a break today... This car was meant for you... Because you're worth it... These homes were built with you in mind... Make your dreams come true...* And so on.

Past experience suggests that when anything becomes all about me, I usually end up sad, mad, or in some sort of trouble. I think that's one of the reasons Jesus challenges us to think just as highly of others—so we won't fall into the pitfalls that come with self-focused living.

It's My (Pity) Party and I'll Cry If I Want To

An unhealthy obsession with self can lead not only to pride but also to self-pity. Many of us have been raised, trained, conditioned, and brainwashed to believe that we are less than, not enough, falling short, failing miserably, and fooling everyone. We carry hidden fears about making the grade, cutting the mustard, and measuring up. We fear being found out and imagine widespread rejection if anyone knew the whole story.

Many of us would benefit from heeding Henri Nouwen's advice on this subject:

For as long as you can remember, you have been a pleaser, depending on others to give you an identity. You need not look at that only in a negative way. You wanted to give your heart to others, and you did so quickly and easily. But now you are being asked to let go of all these self-made props and trust that God is enough for you. You must stop being a pleaser and reclaim your identity as a free self.[1]

Sometimes I (Ellie) suspect that God designs our life experiences just to expose our insecurities and fears and to give us a chance to overcome them with His help. When our third child was born, Frank decided it was time to answer God's call to full-time ministry. Like Sarah with Abraham, I joined my husband in leaving my country (New York), my people (New Yorkers), and my father's household (along with that great Italian food) to trek to the foreign land of Virginia so Frank could accept his new calling as a vice president of Prison Fellowship International.

As for me, I never got a call—or maybe I did and just let it ring. What I did get was a fresh new batch of shame issues each time I encountered the accessorized, shapely, beautiful blond women who seemed to be everywhere I turned. It was enough to make me buy a treadmill. (It makes a great clothing valet.) I felt all alone in my new beige world. Nobody knew me. Nobody cared about my kids. Nobody was interested in my "Ellie-phant" collection. Nobody knew what flavor ice cream I liked most. (Chocolate chip, in case you're wondering.) It was quite a gloomy season for me.

I missed my old church, I missed hosting my radio show, I missed the immediacy with my New York "sistas." I had no history with the people I met, and I lost all my invitations to speak and teach locally. Except for bathing, grocery shopping, and the daily feeding of a man and three offspring, everything familiar came to a screeching halt.

I felt so unsettled by the prefab "planned" town we were living in and the people who would smile and nod but rarely offered opinions, invitations, or hugs. How I longed to return to "the capital of the world," where people are opinionated, aggressive, affectionate, and passionate, and will take you home to share a meal if they like you. I spent my first year in Virginia simmering, seething, and occasionally murmuring under my breath, *Start spreadin' the news... I'm leavin' today...*

If memory serves correctly, I may have vented (or was it dumped?) on my long-suffering husband a few times. You see, I can, on rare occasions (once or twice a day) be erratic, emotional, and rattled. Poor Frank. He is so calm. He is so self-controlled. He is so godly. He is so mellow and even keeled. He is so frustrating, and he was so on my last nerve! (Have I mentioned that I could be a perfect wife if it weren't for Frank?)

We never really fight. We're Christians. But since we're also human and, more to the point, Italian, we occasionally have what you might call "intense fellowship." During one particular time of fellowship, I flailed my arms and loudly protested, "Frank, sometimes you bring out the *worst* in me!"

His response? "Well, honey, I guess it was in there."

I am pleased to report that we celebrated our twenty-fifth wedding anniversary last year. I've grown since those days, and so has he. We get along perfectly now...especially during the weekends...when I'm away.

Even while I was inwardly, and occasionally outwardly, railing about all I'd lost in the move, I knew my attitude was unspiritual, ungrateful, and ungodly. Still, I didn't want to confess that I resented leaving New York and living in northern Virginia. It sounded so immature. It was actually embarrassing to admit to myself (let alone to others) that I was unhappy. The realization that I was behaving in childish, self-absorbed ways saddened my spirit and brought doubts about my self-worth. Between snacks, I often lunched on self-pity, which added to the need for more elastic clothing, which added to other things. It's hard to love yourself when you don't even like yourself.

The good news is that my epiphany eventually occurred. You can read the whole sordid story in my book *Bonding with the Blonde Women*. In a very tiny nutshell, let's just say that it was time to grow up. I realized God's ways are higher than mine, that His timing is just right, and that we should not judge people by their hair color.

Nor should we determine our own worth by how we stack up against others. Romans 12 gives us the following advice:

Do not think of yourself more highly than you ought, but rather think of yourself with sober judgment, in accordance with the measure of faith God has given you. Just as each of us has one body with many members, and these members do not all have the same function, so in Christ we who are many form one body, and each member belongs to all the others. We have different gifts, according to the grace given us. (verses 3–6)

I (Kathy) remember when I first moved to Nashville in 1980. Convinced of my talent, my managers had moved me there from New York in pursuit of a record deal. I sang for anybody and everybody. "We like her voice, but we are not sure how she'll fit in," they would say with a half smile. Comparing myself to the Christian female singers popular at that time, I felt like Rizzo in *Grease*. For the first time in my life I realized I was dark and wore colorful makeup and sounded, well, Italian. I did not blend in! But God had a plan that was perfect for me and my unique gifts. Much to my surprise, my managers decided to start a record company, Reunion Records, with me as their first artist. Here I am twenty-six years later, so blessed to be doing what I do.

Are You Using the Right Mirror?

The more we strive for perfection, the more disappointed and disgusted we become with ourselves. Here's another insightful quote from Henri Nouwen on this subject: "One of the greatest dangers in the spiritual life is self-rejection.... To grow beyond self-rejection we must have the courage to listen to the voice calling us God's beloved sons and daughters, and the determination always to live our lives according to this truth."[2]

Sadly, some of us have a "stepchild" mentality, viewing ourselves as spiritual misfits in the family of God; others are consumed with pride and look down on others as the outsiders. Either state of mind distorts the glorious riches our Father has lavishly given us. It's like being at a carnival and looking in those mirrors that warp and twist your image. How it must break His heart when we don't look at ourselves in the light of His love. Only when we stand before the mirror of His face do we get the clear picture and the eternal perspective that we need while we're here. And only then will we be able to reflect His image to others.

Yet resisting the temptation to compare—and especially to view ourselves as falling short—is not easy, because accusers, yardsticks, scales, and mockers abound. One research study showed that after viewing images in magazine ads for three minutes or less, every woman in the study expressed increased dissatisfaction with her body.[3] Maybe that's one reason behind our national obsession with diets and clothing size. Approximately one in every four college-aged females in America shows symptoms of an eating disorder.[4] We need to remind ourselves that out of four billion females on the planet, only eight are supermodels (give or take a few).

Not only does our culture and the media send distorted messages about beauty, but we're also bombarded with the idea that aging is a fate worse than death. A recent article in *USA Today* declared in bold print "Middle-aged women are less likely to be happy."[5] There was no room for speculation. The research was thorough, and the irrefutable evidence was in. The article was a real downer, thank you very much! Pass us each another slice of chocolate cake.

Messages like these prompt us to view ourselves with a critical eye each time we pass the mirror. *Is that another gray hair? When did those wrinkles appear? Have I gained weight or did I just leave these jeans in the dryer too long?*

All the more reason to remember that the *me* God sees isn't the *me* I see in the mirror. "The LORD does not look at the things man looks at. Man looks at the outward appearance, but the LORD looks at the heart" (1 Samuel 16:7).

The idea of God looking at your heart may be a bit disconcerting in view of those movies that play continually in our minds, reminding us of all the ways we've fallen short in the past and every mistake we've made in the past twenty-four hours. That's why it's so vital to remember that, if you are in Christ, you are a new creation (see 2 Corinthians 5:17). God has given you a brand-new heart (see Ezekiel 36:26). When He looks at you, God sees the bride of Christ—forgiven, holy, honored.

When I (Ellie) look into the mirror of our culture, I will never be satisfied with what I see. But when I look into the mirror of God's Word, I see myself as complete and whole. God calls me blameless, His chosen one, and His child. I am His image bearer. He says that I am a peacemaker and more than a conqueror. He says that I am precious. Isn't that nice? We New Yorkers don't use that word too often, but somehow it sounds right when my heavenly Father calls me *precious*. He sees me and thinks of me as a sweet fragrance, even on days when my attitude stinketh.

Any time I need a reality check, I can turn to the Bible, which says I belong to a royal priesthood. God says I am a runner in His race. He says I am a saint. *Imagine that...me, a saint!* I am the salt of the earth and saved and a servant. I am one of the sheep, and I am a soldier. God also sees me as a work of art. I am so glad that the Master Painter continues to add His brush strokes upon my heart.

The desire to change, to improve isn't wrong in itself. In fact, the Christian life is all about change. But lasting beauty can't be found in a jar or tube. And our worth isn't based on our special talents or hard work. We become women of irresistible beauty and confidence when we stop hiding behind shame or bravado and step out into the light, inviting God to reach into the broken, messy places of our souls and touch them with His love.

Letting Go of Perfection

What sweet peace comes from knowing that God loves us fully and completely, no matter what we did yesterday or nineteen years ago. That does not mean that our choices don't have consequences. Indeed they do. However, the repentant heart is free to fly toward forgiveness, healing, and living a satisfied life filled with joy and purpose.

Jesus extends an irresistible invitation to all who are tired of carrying guilt, shame, and other unwanted baggage: "Come to me, all you who are weary and burdened, and I will give you rest. Take my yoke upon you and learn from me, for I am gentle and humble in heart, and you will find rest for your souls. For my yoke is easy and my burden is light" (Matthew 11:28–30).

The Lord invites us to lay it all down and rip that big *S* off our chests. None of us look quite right in Superwoman's boots anyway.

Of course, one of the key reasons God puts other people in our lives is to lift our spirits and help ease our burdens. Part of loving ourselves means being honest enough to ask for help when we need it rather than pressing ahead to the point of exhaustion. Whether it's asking the family to pitch in around the house, letting Daddy enjoy some quality time with the kids during an occasional girls' night out, or just opening up to a trusted and wise counselor, each of us needs to resist our compulsion to handle life on our own. And we need to respond with humility, gratitude, and a resounding "Yes!" when a perceptive friend offers her help in practical, sanity-preserving ways.

I (Kathy) am so thankful for my close friends. I have carefully picked each one and have pursued honesty and openness with them. In return they have been authentic and candid with me.

Let's *Dish* About...
Adjusting the Mirror

EL: Kathy, when you realize you're getting a bit down on yourself, how do you adjust your perspective?

KT: I've had great practice at this! I can't tell you how often I host private little "Kathy Troccoli is not so holy" parties. Each time, I have to go back to God's love and tenderness and what He says about me. I return often to my favorite story in Scripture, about Mary of Bethany and how Jesus let her radically worship Him and stay at His feet when everyone else thought she was out of her mind. His grace is so unfathomable. I adore Him for that. I also find it helpful to occasionally pick up the phone and ask one of my close friends to tell me what she sees in me that's good and true. I know I won't get hype but powerful words of hope.

EL: It's so easy for me to engage in negative self-talk: "You're a loser. You blew it. You'll never get organized. You're not as intelligent as she is…" and on it goes. But it is an affront to the Father when I cast aspersions upon myself. It is only Satan who sneers and sits in agreement with such hurtful judgments and accusations.

I try to remember an expression that is often used in prison ministry: "God doesn't make junk." I know the Lord is good, mighty, lovely, and kind, and I remind myself that I am made in His image. I am His workmanship, His masterpiece, His beloved. I am fearfully and wonderfully made. I am an overcomer. I can do all things through Christ who strengthens me. When I turn my eyes upon Jesus, I can then see myself as He sees me…as a precious jewel, not discarded junk.

You need to work on that.
That person isn't good for you.
You need to change that.
That is unacceptable at this point in your life.
I would really think about it before you make that call.
Erase that e-mail. Don't send it.

I may not always love hearing the truth but, boy, does it breed good things in me. Integrity and virtue and substance come from being challenged—listening, sorting, accepting, and rising to the occasion.

I have often said that there is no joyride to holiness, but when we are open to receiving God's love, wisdom, and rebuke in the ways that He desires to send them, we can't help but become more like Jesus. I am not the woman I was twenty years ago. Not the one I was ten, or even five, years ago. I pray I will have more attributes of Jesus Christ in my character with every passing year. But that only happens as I let go of my illusions of independence and rely increasingly on Him.

When we repent of our exhausting self-sufficiency and make a 180-degree turn, then God begins to guide our speech, our thoughts, our actions, and yes— He even redefines our self-worth. Brennan Manning said,

> Self-acceptance is the experience of salvation rooted in the acceptance of
> Jesus Christ on Calvary. And when we surrender with childlike confidence
> and trust that Jesus accepts us as we are—even in our sinfulness—that
> becomes the root of our own self-acceptance. Then, paradoxically, we are
> free to forget ourselves and turn our eyes toward Jesus and other people.[6]

Isn't it interesting how it's all tangled up together like strands of spaghetti? As we accept God's love for us, we achieve a healthy grasp of loving ourselves and are fully freed to love Him in return, which then propels us to invest our lives in loving others.

The talented, albeit tragic, rocker Janis Joplin once said, "Today is the first day of the rest of your life." Why not begin today to love yourself the way God loves you? The Christian life is one of new beginnings. The curtain rises at the start of a new day. You are not the woman you once were, and God stands ready to shape you into the woman you are meant to be—a woman who practices humility and obtains honor, a woman who values sacrifice and enjoys celebration, a woman who is meek in spirit and mighty in faith.

God will continue to make all things new just as He said.

Remember, the best makeovers happen from the inside out.

Thoughts to *Noodle* On

1. Think of a woman you know who exudes true inside-out beauty. To what would you attribute her attractiveness?

2. What are some areas in which you might be tempted to think too highly of yourself? In what areas do you tend to be overly critical of yourself?

3. As you consider how God describes you in His Word— forgiven, holy, honored—what shifts do you sense within your heart?

4. As you look back over the past few years, can you identify at least one way in which God is changing you for the better? If so, explain the changes you've noticed. If not, in what area will you invite Him to reach in and perform a makeover?

Dolce ▪ Dessert

Savor Every Bite

All things are possible to one who believes;
even more to one who hopes; still more to
one who loves, and even more to one who
perseveres in the practice of these three virtues.

—BROTHER LAWRENCE

How Sweet It Is

*n*o matter how long you sit around the Italian table, no matter how full you feel, no matter how tight your waistband has become, there is *always* room for dessert. Even the dieters, moderate eaters, and those blessed with slight waistlines are somehow goaded or guilted into this last lap of gastric indulgence. It is heralded by the distinctive aroma of the espresso beans and the whizzing sound of the cappuccino machine, which serves as the curtain call for the final act.

Dessert is the apex, the grand finale, the epicurean Alps. It brings the joy of being transported to a higher realm. We call it *dolce.*

To our mutual regret, genuine Italian *pasticcerias* (pastry shops) and *panetterias* (bread shops) are rare to nonexistent in the south, at least in the areas where we each live. Although our grandmothers, mothers, and aunts certainly knew how to whip up scrumptious delights, neither of us is especially skilled in creating Italian meals, let alone genuine homemade desserts. For too many reasons to list here, we prefer to be consumers rather than creators. (Not to worry; the recipes we have shared are fabulous. We promise.)

For that reason, whenever we visit our families in New York or when we joyfully find ourselves in the Italian section of a city, we become misty eyed about the anticipated fare. When the dessert options are discussed, we find it too difficult to choose, so we have adopted the regular habit of Frank Lofaro, which is to buy one different dessert for each guest and pass them around the table. Every sixty seconds you pass the plate clockwise and keep your fork. That is *our* version of happy hour!

And what exactly would be circling around the table? *Cannoli, pizzelle, spumoni, tortoni, biscotti, pignoli torta, panettone, tiramisu, sfogliatelle, torrone, Baci*—if you don't know what these are, you need to get out and get personal with a good Italian restaurant. And this all comes *after* the fruit and nuts. We love to taste everything and to savor every bite.

So too the person who feasts on faith, hope, and love will find great delight in savoring *la dolce vita,* the sweet life. You don't need to be from any particular ethnic group, religious denomination, or economic stratum to enjoy the abundant life

Phyllis's Angelloni Cookies

The perfect after-dinner sweet treat, great with coffee, cappuccino, or ice-cold milk.

Ingredients

- 1 cup butter-flavored Crisco
- 1 cup sugar
- 3 eggs
- zest from 1 lemon
- 2 teaspoons baking powder
- juice of 1 lemon
- 2 1/2 cups flour

Icing ingredients (optional, see below)
- 1 cup powdered sugar
- juice of 1 more lemon

Cooking Instructions

1. Preheat oven to 350 degrees.

that God so freely gives to those who seek Him. Jesus's offer is available to anyone who believes His promise: "I am the bread of life. He who comes to me will never go hungry, and he who believes in me will never be thirsty" (John 6:35).

When you partake in a steady diet of Jesus and His Word, the sweet fruit of His presence will permeate every aspect of your being. You'll exude an aliveness of the soul that demonstrates vitality, passion, and purpose.

What happens when we live God's way? He brings gifts into our lives, much the same way that fruit appears in an orchard—things like affection for others, exuberance about life, serenity. We develop a willingness to stick

2. With electric beater, mix sugar and Crisco. Adding one egg at a time, beat until smooth. Add lemon zest, juice of 1 lemon, and baking powder; mix with a spoon while gradually adding flour. Stir batter until it has a sticky consistency, like peanut butter.

3. Flour your fingers, roll dough into walnut-size balls, and place on an ungreased cookie sheet. Bake for approximately 12 to 15 minutes, until bottoms are lightly browned.

4. If desired, ice cooled cookies as follows: Place 1 cup powdered sugar in a small bowl. Stir in one teaspoon lemon juice, then continue adding very small amounts of lemon juice (approximately one teaspoon at a time) until icing has a thick, smooth consistency; it should not be soupy. When cookies have cooled, dunk each, topside down, in icing and place on cookie sheet until icing dries.

5. Enjoy!

Yields approximately 3 to 4 dozen cookies.

with things, a sense of compassion in the heart, and a conviction that a basic holiness permeates things and people. We find ourselves involved in loyal commitments, not needing to force our way in life, able to marshal and direct our energies wisely. (Galatians 5:22–23, MSG)

We have met the victorious woman who possesses a countenance of angelic beauty. Her face is lined with fierce strength, and yet she exudes tenderness, kindness, and a love that invites you in. When you are near her, you feel not only welcomed but also sheltered with care. You are in the presence of grace. She is a friend of God, well acquainted with His Word. She knows who she is and whose she is. She does not know what the future holds, but she knows who holds the future. She laughs easily and often. She fills up on faith, hope, and love, and she delights in the sweetness of God's companionship at the table.

We have met the scarred woman who has been tested by life's fires, floods, and storms. Through it all, she has undeniably placed her hope in Christ alone. She is strong with wisdom and robust with integrity. You want to sit and listen and glean insight from this gentle warrior who has kept her eyes on God no matter the circumstances. Her hardships have not made her bitter or callous; her private tears have actually made her sweeter and softer. She understands that God has the final word in every situation, and though life seems unfair, she looks forward to the time when every tear will be wiped away. She fills up on faith, hope, and love, and she savors the sweetness of knowing the best is yet to come.

We have met the tireless woman who is God's handmaiden. She finds purpose and joy in taking care of the needs of her family, but she doesn't keep her gifts hidden within the walls of her home. She gives her life away at the homeless shelter, the nursing home, or the HIV clinic. She offers grace and peace to the other parents she meets at the PTA, the 4-H Club, or the children's program at church. She invites the neighborhood kids to hang out in her yard and home, nourishing both their bodies and souls. She doesn't wonder what Jesus would do; she just does it. Her service to others brings great joy, and the more she gives her life away, the more she finds it. Her smile is contagious, and her readiness to offer hugs brings healing to those who don't even realize how deeply they ache for a gentle touch. She fills up on faith, hope, and love, and she finds sweet joy in welcoming others to the table.

We have met the single woman whose confidence is based on the words of Isaiah: "Your Maker is your husband" (54:5). Even though she may feel lonely some days, she remains secure in the fact that she is never alone. She is surrounded by rich relationships, and her heart is full because she has poured herself out. When she ponders her legacy, she knows that the chapters of her life tell a story of the eternal mark she is making on this world. She treasures the precious time she has alone with God, and she structures her life around the purpose of making the gospel both her comfort and her cause. She fills up on faith, hope, and love, and then she serves generous heapings to those in need.

Each of these women has discovered that Jesus is the Giver and Perfecter of faith, hope, and love. When you are fed at His table, you will surely become a living vessel whom He can bless others through.

Live a lover's life, circumspect and exemplary, a life Jesus will be proud of: bountiful in fruits from the soul, making Jesus Christ attractive to all, getting everyone involved in the glory and praise of God. (Philippians 1:9–11, MSG)

It is our fervent prayer that you would never settle for the crumbs of this workaday, "give it your best shot," "just hang in there" world. We pray that you will resist the junk food of life, that you'll refuse to settle for the thin gruel of sadness and isolation, and that you'll decline to overindulge in those things that weigh you down with shame. Instead come join us at God's table and continue to feast on all that is eternal.

Only three things will last.

Only three things matter.

Only three things will bring you home.

These three will remain: *faith, hope,* and *love.*

Come to the table...

Let the Feast Continue!

We hope you'll find opportunities to use one or more of the terrific recipes we've included in this book. We truly are passionate about Italian food. But let's face it, most of us do not have the time in the kitchen that our grandmothers did. That's why we've provided a list of our favorite Web sites featuring Italian recipes, genuine products, fun facts, and endless inspiration. We invite you to explore and discover more of the *delizioso* specialties that await your senses.

Remember, to create the best Italian dish, you need to use the best Italian ingredients. So at these Web sites you'll find what you need to get cooking or have the whole meal delivered. Happy surfing!

www.alescifoods.com	*best* deli
www.annamariavolpi.com	recipes with step-by-step photos
www.cento.com	fine imported food
www.ferraracafe.com	*best* pastries and cookies
www.ibfoods.com	gift baskets
www.ditalia.com	imported food
www.initaly.com	products and recipes
www.italianfinefood.com	recipes
www.italianfood.about.com	recipes
www.italianfoodforever.com	article, journals, recipes
www.italianchef.com	all things Italian
www.italiansrus.com	culture, traditions, more
www.italyum.com	recipes
www.moltobuono.com	ingredients
www.peruginachocolate.com	*best* chocolate
www.rosafoods.com	*best* pizza sauce
www.torronecandy.com	*best* candy
www.victoriapacking.com	*best* jar sauce

Notes

Chapter 1

1. Augustine, *A Select Library of the Nicene and Post-Nicene Fathers of the Christian Church,* vol. 7, *St. Augustin: Homilies on the Gospel of John; Homilies on the First Epistle of John; Soliloquies,* ed. Philip Schaff (New York: Christian Literature, 1886; Peabody, MA: Hendrickson, 1995), Tractate 29, 184.

Chapter 3

1. Augustine, *A Select Library of the Nicene and Post-Nicene Fathers of the Christian Church,* vol. 3, *St. Augustin: On the Holy Trinity; Doctrinal Treatises; Moral Treatises,* ed. Philip Schaff (New York: Christian Literature, 1887; Peabody, MA: Hendrickson, 1995), 528.
2. Hal Borland, *Beyond Your Doorstep: A Handbook to the Country* (Guilford, CT: Globe Pequot, 2003), 75.
3. Adapted from Lisa Beamer, *Let's Roll! Ordinary People, Extraordinary Courage* (Wheaton, IL: Tyndale, 2002), 212.
4. Amy Carmichael, *Things As They Are: Mission Work in Southern India* (London: Morgan and Scott, 1903), 158.

Chapter 4

1. Edward Mote, "The Solid Rock," circa 1834. Public domain.
2. Frederick Buechner, *The Final Beast* (New York: Atheneum, 1965; San Francisco: Harper & Row, 1982), 175.
3. Ken Gire, *The North Face of God* (Wheaton, IL: Tyndale, 2005), 120.
4. Corrie ten Boom, quoted in Pamela Rosewell Moore, *Life Lessons from the Hiding Place* (Grand Rapids: Chosen Books, 2004), 74.
5. Amy Carmichael, *Rose from Brier* (Fort Wayne, PA: Christian Literature Crusade, 1972).

Chapter 5

1. C. S. Lewis, *Mere Christianity* (New York: HarperCollins, 2001), 136–37.
2. Billy Graham, *Breakfast with Billy Graham* (New York: Testament Books/ Random House Value, 1996), 97.
3. Jerry Bridges, *I Will Follow You, O God* (Colorado Springs: WaterBrook, 2001), 44.

Chapter 6

1. Luis Palau, *Where Is God When Bad Things Happen?* (New York: Galilee/ Doubleday, 1999), 40.

Chapter 7

1. Frederick M. Lehman, "The Love of God," 1917. Public domain.

Chapter 8

1. Alfred Williams Momerie, *Defects of Modern Christianity and Other Sermons* (Edinburgh and London: Blackwood, 1882), 66–67.
2. Emily Dickinson, *Poems by Emily Dickinson, Series One* (Project Gutenberg, 2000), http://infomotions.com/etexts/gutenberg/dirs/etext01/1mlyd10.htm. Public domain.
3. John Barnett, *Revelation: From Now to Forever* (Tulsa, OK: BFM, 2004), 457.
4. John R. Rice, *Golden Moments with Dr. John R. Rice* (Murfreesboro, TN: Sword of the Lord, 1977), 183.

Chapter 10

1. Henri J. M. Nouwen, *The Inner Voice of Love* (New York: Image/Doubleday, 1998), 5.
2. Henri J. M. Nouwen, *The Dance of Life*, ed. Michael Ford (Notre Dame, IN: Ave Maria, 2005), 118.
3. University of Missouri News Bureau, "Women of all sizes feel badly about their bodies after seeing models," news release, 26 March 2007.
4. Carolyn Costin, *Eating Disorder Sourcebook* (Los Angeles: Lowell, 1999), 19.

5. Marilyn Elias, "Middle-aged women are less likely to be happy," *USA Today,* 12 November 2006.

6. Paula Rinehart, "Living as God's Beloved: An Interview with Brennan Manning," *Discipleship Journal* 100 (July/August 1997), 72.

Are You *Missing Out* on the *Joy* and *Adventure* of *Life?*

Don't wait another day. Dare to reach beyond mere routine and grab hold of a rich, passionate life.

Available in bookstores and from online retailers.